Silent
Storm

Silent Storm

Finding Spiritual Shelter During Hepatitis C

by **Mark Prater**

with C.L. Carden

FOREWORD BY NAOMI JUDD

new
hope
PUBLISHERS

Birmingham, Alabama

New Hope® Publishers
P.O. Box 12065
Birmingham, AL 35202-2065
www.newhopepublishers.com

Library of Congress Cataloging-in-Publication Data
Prater, Mark.
Silent storm : finding spiritual shelter during hepatitis C / by Mark Prater with C.L. Carden ; foreword by Naomi Judd.
p. cm.
ISBN 1-56309-900-4 (softcover)
1.   Hepatitis C-Patients-Religious life. 2. Hepatitis C-Religious aspects-Christianity. 3. Prater, Mark. I. Carden, C. L. II. Title.
BV4910.6.H44P73 2005
248.8'61963623—dc22
2004025988

ISBN: 1-56309-900-4
N054105 • 0305 • 6M1

Dedication

To my children, wife, parents, brothers, and sisters, who have shown me what unconditional love is... and to Jesus Christ for giving His life for mine.
*—**Mark Prater***

To Johanna, Yasmin, Serina, and Ellen V.M. Carden, and Margery W. Brown, who are, respectively, my life, my love, and my inspiration.
*—**C.L. Carden***

Table of Contents

Foreword

by Naomi Judd

Oh no, another person with hepatitis C, I thought as the request came in for me to make a phone call to a fellow down South. *How unfortunate that the number of requests for me to talk to people with hep C is increasing. It's becoming unmanageable,* I thought. But because it is so important for anyone who's suffering to be able to connect with another person who has been through their issue, I made time to call this fellow named Mark Prater.

Shortly after our one-on-one conversation began, however, I knew this was not the typical hep C patient. As a professional member of the broadcast media, well-known in his region, he was struggling with a dilemma known only to public figures. He had a desire to spread information and awareness about hepatitis C, yet felt a fear of negative stereotyping. "Mark," I advised him, "you're the only one who can come to this decision, but the only way we can destigmatize hep C is for you and people like you to educate the public about it."

I was a nurse before Wynonna and I got into country music. My hepatitis C was probably incurred by a contaminated needle stick from a patient I took care of in ICU in the early '80s. I have never been drunk and am monogamous—thereby blowing to bits the stereotype that liver disease is only a result of alcoholism or promiscuous behavior.

It's important that we understand how widespread hepatitis C is. Hepatitis C is four times more common than HIV. Few of the people who have the virus know that they have it. By the time they realize they have it, many people with hep C have extensive liver damage. Former U.S. Surgeon General C. Everett Koop says that viral hepatitis is one of the most significant treatable and preventable public health problems facing the U.S. today. He says that unless something is done soon, hepatitis C will kill far more people each year than AIDS.

It's important that we realize there are many ways to get hepatitis C. Hepatitis simply refers to an inflammation of the liver. For instance, the suffix -itis at the end of a word just means "inflammation of," as in tonsillitis, bronchitis, appendicitis. Hepat is the medical term for liver. We need to let people know there are multiple causes for inflammation of our liver. Some causes can be mechanical, like plumbing obstructions. Another cause can be an accumulation of iron in the bloodstream (hemochromatosis). Inflammation can be stirred up because the liver is the ultimate filter for the body. A person who is painting inside a closed room might suffer from paint fumes or be exposed to caustic inhalation that may hurt their liver. Obviously, illegal drugs and prescription medications, if taken inappropriately, can put stress and strain on the liver as it tries to detoxify one's system. Then, of course, there are bacterial and viral pathogens. There are hepatitis A, hepatitis B, hepatitis C, and, in fact, other alphabetically noted viral forms.

As Mark shared his personal experience with me, I was struck by his deep and abiding Christian faith. I breathed a sigh of relief. He understood that we are first and foremost spiritual beings having a human experience. It's not really what happens to us, whether it's hep C or any catastrophe; it's really how we deal with it. I felt certain this would become a voyage of self-discovery on his journey to wholeness.

One of the things I learned in my own research of the last decade into how people heal is that each of us must figure out our own life story. We must become detectives in our lives. We must clean up past trauma, since it is actually encoded on a cellular level. What we believe can make us sick! We must let go of the past and release negativity and unhealthy beliefs. Our body's innate immune system must become mobilized to keep the virus from multiplying and to quell it.

Having been convinced by experts in medicine, psychology, and science that our beliefs indeed become our biology, I explained to Mark that the brain is an organ like the liver. The brain is a three-pound tangible object. It's tantamount to a drugstore. It manufactures and releases all sorts of hormones and biochemicals known as neuropeptides. The mind, however, is the body's information pathway. It's invisible, but you can think of it as the body's control tower. You control your mind. You control your thoughts. When you tell yourself that your illness is an opportunity to learn more about yourself, to understand more completely your oneness with God, you tell your brain to manufacture and secrete beneficial neuropeptides like serotonin and dopamine. Failure to understand or acknowledge this reality of the mind/body connection results in a decreased immune response. It can either cause an illness, or prevent one from healing.

Having studied with brainiacs in the spirit/mind/body fields, I have put my findings into my book, *Naomi's Breakthrough Guide: 20 Choices to Transform Your Life.* The book is a self-portrait of how I healed and even was ultimately cured. Revelations include the understanding that when we can't control our circumstances (a grim diagnosis for any problem), we still have the power to choose our reaction, and that's everything. The way we choose to react determines happiness versus unhappiness, or sometimes literally life versus death.

Another concept is that illness provides an opportunity to evaluate that something is out of balance in our life. The body wants to be whole and healthy. When we stuff our emotions, refusing to acknowledge or deal with them, the body takes over. The body manifests unresolved conflict. Although Mark was ill and was obviously hit by a tsunami of lifestyle dilemmas (such as whether he would be able to work and provide for his family, how this would affect his marriage, indeed all of his relationships, and so on), I felt a spiritual maturity in him that I knew would eventually be the greatest medicine.

One of the blessings of my life is the opportunity to travel extensively. When I launched my book tour in January of 2004, I eagerly looked forward to meeting Mark at the TV studio, where I could catch up on his progress. To my delight, I felt I'd known him forever. As we visited

on-camera at the TV studio, I was enormously proud that
he had made the compassionate decision to use his visibility
to put a face and a personal story on this silent killer.
"There's no such thing as a coincidence," I remarked. "It's
just God's way of staying invisible." This was all part of a
divine plan. It's through our personal stories that we connect. This gives us an opportunity to learn to also love our
story and to understand that as we share our unique experience with another, we gain insights and learn more. For
instance, as I watched Mark—and Mark's body language—
as he told his story, I saw that he had a curiosity about life,
and the trait of courage. After the televised interview, an
unusually pretty brunette introduced herself as Mark's wife.
As we visited, it was made evident once again that any illness or crisis affects the entire family.

You are a unique and special individual. The fact that
you have this book tells me you're a seeker, that you intend
to become proactive in your life. I encourage you to gather
all the information available. Find "Dr. Right"—that physician who will become your partner in this journey. Use this
as an opportunity to learn more about your beliefs. Learn
your story and then tell it to someone else. If information is
our most valuable tool in dealing with any reality, self-
knowledge is the sledgehammer.

God be with Mark and his family, and may the anoint-
ing of the Holy Spirit be upon this book. All is well.

Chapter One
Discovery

For thou hast been a strength to the poor, a strength
to the needy in his distress, a refuge from the storm.
—Isaiah 25: 4

Children turn their faces to the sky and in the clouds they see mythical shapes, the shapes of angels, the outlines of dreams pushed by the wind into memories. Looking into the sky over Prattville, Alabama, I imagined I saw my father's wings. I used to look for his Air Force bird, and his obsession with the sky became my own.

When I became a man I learned to see other things in the sky: the curl of a breeze and what it meant by the way it brushed across my face. As a television meteorologist I learned to see into the future, a fortuneteller with better toys. I listened to the weather watchers—Hamm radio operators with their eyes to the sky—scouting for ice or damaging winds. I learned to read Doppler radar and the telltale hooks of F5 tornadoes. I can tell what's coming by the smell of the air or the electric velvet feel of the atmosphere heralding a storm. I can literally smell danger. I'm used to knowing what's going to happen before everyone else. I can tell you if it is going to rain, or if the sun will bless you with rays of hope, or if you will wake up under a thick blanket of snow. I can tell you if your home is in the path of a merciless storm and whether you should hunker down in the storm cellar or run for your life. At the Birmingham, Alabama television station ABC 33/40, it is my job. I'm not always right. But I'm hardly ever wrong. Forecasting the weather isn't guesswork; it's like learning to read. Once you learn the language and see the signs, the hard work is finished.

But life has its own mysterious language, and anyone who thinks he or she can see what's coming is second-guessing God. I could not have guessed that the wind and rain and the sky that I loved would lead me into a successful, award-winning television career that would take me places I hadn't imagined. I could not have known that my notion of happiness as a young man would be turned on its ear by the woman I asked to be my wife, or that she would accept. I could not have guessed that as my life went along, as I met challenges and overcame them, raising a family and building a career, that I was harboring a potential killer, or that I would not face my greatest challenge until the killer finally showed its face.

Personal Hurricane

I contracted hepatitis C on a day I could have easily died. It stayed with me for years afterward, but it hid inside me like a coward, biding its time. When it was ready it came out fighting, and in the battle to cure myself of it there were times when I honestly wished that God would ease my suffering and call me home. But my disease would never completely win, because it was alone and I had my strength, and my wife Carol's strength, and our children, and my faith in God, against all of which nothing can stand.

It is easy now to imagine that my fight against hepatitis C was being waged in the midst of a personal hurricane. For six months I stood in the center of a whirlwind of pain, disorientation, and emotional distress. I fought to stand, and often I fell, neither willing nor able to rise to my feet. Real hurricanes often leave the towns in their path broken and weeping. But the towns find strength to recover. That's what fighting hepatitis C is like.

Maybe it is better that I found out about my disease after I became a man, instead of as a boy chasing his father's wings. I had risen to an enviable height in my career and my personal life had fallen in line—a beautiful home, four wonderful, cherubic children, and a woman whom I adored. I stood on the peak of personal and professional success, which also meant that I had a long way to fall. I refused to go down easily. It is not in my personality. But I took a lot of lumps along the way.

On the Air

Broadcasters are like dedicated theatrical performers. Before a show, we rehearse our lines. We perfect our four-in-hand knots and apply our makeup with care. On the air, we project our voices like stage actors, as if we aren't being helped by broadcast equipment worth millions of dollars. If we catch a cold, we don't walk to the pharmacy, we run— because a bad cold can take us off the air for several days, a cardinal sin in the business. We charge off to work, lock ourselves in our offices, and gulp herbal tea and cold remedies until we've successfully masked any sign of illness. On with the show.

But in January 2002, I was losing a long battle with what I thought was a common cold—a particularly nasty, unrelenting cold, but a common one nonetheless. It came with all the right symptoms: a persistent cough, fatigue, sinus problems, and a slow deterioration of my voice. I'd been living with these symptoms for months, writing them off as allergies. But the effect the symptoms were having on me was becoming pretty evident during news broadcasts, and it became impossible to ignore.

Typically, I'd begin with a look at the national forecast and then spend a minute or more on regional developments, all the while battling a murky cough. By the time I reached the seven-day forecast, I'd sound as if I was delivering the news from the bottom of the sea. It was my voice alone that informed millions of viewers during those morning segments as I flew solo between commercial breaks, and if my voice cracked, rattled, or broke down completely, people noticed.

One of the people who noticed was the man who keeps me employed, the station's news director, Garry Kelly. Garry is a sweetheart of a guy whose natural inclination to help is constantly at war with his responsibility to grind his staff into paste in the quest for quality ratings. It's the news business, and no one gets ahead by playing nicely. After watching a few disastrous performances, Garry brought me into his office, shaking his great shock of salt and pepper hair. "Your voice sounds terrible. What's going on?" he asked. I explained, grunting and hacking up half a lung, so that at the end of it he relented and told me to take the rest of the day off. We had a number of one-sided conversations like this that usually ended with Garry telling me to shut up and go home in his oddly sympathetic way, but it was clear to Garry that something should be done

One of the other people who noticed my voice was Dr. Carl Nechtman, M.D., an otolaryngologist to whom I went to straighten things out. I made the first of four visits to him at Birmingham's HealthSouth Medical Center, a sprawling, modern behemoth of steel and smoked glass. It has the feel of a well-run bank with all the warmth of an underground vault. Thank God for Carl.

Carl Nechtman started out as my doctor. He became my friend. In between, he helped save my life, for which I will never adequately be able to repay him. He is perhaps the most comfortable person I know, and one of the best informed. Information rolls off of him in waves and he drowned me in it, answering every pointless, stupid question I asked with more patience than I could have reasonably expected. Gentle and at ease, he approached my sinus and throat problems with an attention to detail that would prove to be crucial later on.

I was introduced to Carl by a friend and fellow broadcaster, Bill "Bubba" Bussey, of the syndicated morning-drive radio show, the Rick and Bubba Show. Dr. Nechtman successfully solved Bill's serious snoring problem with nasal surgery. But the fact that Dr. Nechtman was personally recommended to me didn't mean that I was eager to visit. To me, a visit to the doctor is as fulfilling as emptying the trash or mowing the lawn—a necessary evil to be put off as long as possible. I was feeling run down and beat up. I slept sometimes 17 hours a day and I'd still wake up tired. In the end there was no escaping the quality of my voice. No voice means no job. No job puts Carol and the kids on the bread line. So I summoned my will and prayed that a shot of B-12 and a steroid would work wonders on my pipes.

Carl started small, concluding, as I suspected, that I had a viral syndrome or a moderate cold. At first he prescribed decongestants and cough medicine, which had no effect. I couldn't shake it, and reluctantly I went to him again. I had convinced myself that it was just a tough cold. What else could it have been? The symptoms came and went. There were days when I almost felt normal, and on those days I would be fooled into thinking I was cured. But inevitably the laryngitis and the fatigue would return. I went back to Carl, but the results of the treatments remained negligible. By the fourth trip in three months to see him, the good doctor began to show some concern.

Carl had thrown everything at me he could think of to treat my aches and pains. Bottom line, I wasn't responding to what would seem like adequate treatment for the diagnosis. Still, I was prepared for a final visit and some magic concoction to get me back on the air in top shape. Instead, Carl looked me in the eye. A fan of my TV and radio show appearances, he had noticed the quality of my voice going from bad to worse over the course of several weeks. He was insistent. "Mark, you're not getting any better. I'm going to ask you to let me do some blood work."

Blood work. It was like he was speaking a different language. How could blood work resolve a scratchy throat and a cough? Then I had a flash of darkness, a swift, subconscious premonition of fear and pain. There was no organized thought attached to it, but if the feeling could have been put into words, they would have been, *Oh no, this is bad.*

What I actually said was, "Let me give it some time." I wasn't ready for a blood test or what it would mean. I managed to convince myself that it was a harmless condition that would work itself out, no tests needed. I stonewalled Dr. Nechtman and he knew it.

In my mind I already had it figured out. The first three months of the year are the busiest for me. The station has the weather team doing storm tours, where we visit different cities and take our forecasting on the road. In addition, I get booked for 150 to 200 speaking engagements at schools and civic centers annually. At the time, I was sleeping no more than five hours a night and I was pushing harder and harder at work covering severe weather. Dr. Nechtman had also put me on a diet regimen, urging me to drop 15 pounds. The answer seemed obvious to me. I was run down and worn out and my body was catching up to me. I ducked his phone calls and stalled for time. But the good doctor also knew better than to try to convince me. He went to the one person who can bend my will with a word. He called Carol. "He's got to come in," he told my wife. "Make him come in."

Carol cornered me after work and fixed me with one of those looks she gives to the kids at bedtime. "All right, look. Dr. Nechtman has set this up so all you have to do is walk in, get the needle stuck in your arm, and walk out. Go get it done." I don't argue with Carol. On her first hunting trip in college she bagged a six-point buck. Its head hangs on the wall in our family room as a warning.

I hustled to Carl's office between shows, and as promised Carl had greased the wheels for me. The paperwork was prepared for my signature; his nurse slipped me out the rear door of his office and walked me down to the lab on the second floor. The test would check my electrolytes, blood counts, and liver enzymes, which would give Carl a better understanding of what we were facing. I exchanged some quiet words with the lab personnel before I was jabbed, bandaged, and sent on my way. I was glad to put the whole episode behind me and I went back to my hectic schedule. My symptoms had even lessened. I don't think I thought about it once in between the time that I had the blood drawn and the moment he called.

My test results showed an elevated level of liver enzymes, markers for conditions that fall out of Dr. Nechtman's realm of expertise. Carl, in an act as unselfish and as humble as they come, recommended that I see a colleague. "Look," he said calmly, "we've got a problem here, but I want to send you to someone else who is more experienced in the field treating something like this. I'm an ear, nose and throat guy—probably the best ear doctor in town. But this is something a specialist needs to check."

It would have been easy to put him off again, and run away from the possibility of any bad news. But how far could I run? I didn't know what I was looking at. Cancer? HIV? The greatest fear is of the unknown, so running was not an option. It was time to take the thief's mask off.

Carl and Carol began the careful search for a specialist. Fortunately, Carol had a childhood friend who was an internist in Birmingham; he was willing to see me on short notice. After booking the appointment with Dr. Chris Black, we were in and drawing blood again.

Dr. Black and Carol knew each other through the connections people make in very small towns, though they hadn't had contact in years. He had dated one of her girl-friends, and their families lived near each other. Of course, in tiny Monroeville, Alabama, everybody in town lives nearby.

Diagnosis

Chris is a graying, soft-spoken professional who inspires confidence. He asked a lot of questions and did the blood work to see what exactly put Carl on alert. After seeing in the results the elevated enzyme levels Carl saw, he ordered another test, this one intended to detect hepatitis. Carol and I quietly decided that hepatitis was a remote possibility, primarily because we knew nothing about it. The people who usually contracted hepatitis, we believed, were drug users and other unsavory types. That was how naïve we were. The only person I knew who had ever acquired it otherwise was my good friend Scott Dawson, an evangelist, who got it through contaminated food.

By the time I was having my blood drawn and tested, Scott had recovered from hepatitis A. I remember watching him struggle to maintain a regular life. He worked hard to keep up appearances and often took to bed, fulfilling his need for bed rest. In truth I felt sorry for him, never knowing that I would soon be taking a similar path. The disease sounded vile, and I was thankful he'd come through, and more than a little relieved that I had my health.

Carol and I did know enough about hepatitis to know that it could cause serious liver damage, including cirrhosis, and could lead to liver failure and death. The virus could go undetected for decades. By the time symptoms are noticed, the virus could have done significant damage to the liver.

And there is no vaccine for hepatitis C.

Chris Black was out of town when I went back for the test results. A partner in the medical office filling in for him confirmed there was indeed a problem and that it could be a form of hepatitis. More tests were needed.

The processing of blood work takes longer than you might expect. One week slipped by and then another and in the meantime my anxieties nearly fell away. I kept busy. I'd kept the tests to myself, so no one asked questions about them. I played golf when I could squeeze in a few rounds. I played with the kids. Same old jovial Mark, delivering the forecast with a grin and a couple of bad jokes tossed in for good measure.

I came home one day in a good mood and washed away the studio makeup, making the quick transition from Mark Prater, meteorologist, into Just Plain Mark, Dad and Hubby. As usual, Carol came into the bathroom behind me. Often, she's interested in my day and she will ask about how the show went. More often than not, she will run down the list of jobs that need my attention around the house. She'll even joke that after a day at home with the kids it is a relief to have a conversation that doesn't include mashed peas or diapers. But she was quiet. She has an expressive face, an easy smile. But the expression she wore at that moment was rigid, as if she'd been too long in the winter wind.

"I got a call today from the doctor," she said. "Your tests are in."

I managed to turn and hang up my suit. For someone expecting to hear the worst, I was composed and confident. I smiled bravely and said, "So what have they got for me?" I watched her face and the tremendous effort she put forth to hold it together, an early sign of the strength she would show over the coming months.

"I'm so sorry, honey. You're infected with hepatitis C, Mark."

Someone once remarked that absolute silence is deafening. I was overwhelmed by the absence of noise, movement, time, and feeling. The shock of it shut me down as if someone had turned off the lights, closed the door, and locked me up tight. I thought, *Lord help me, I'm going to die. I'm 33 years old, and I'm finished.* I took Carol in my arms and tried to support her with strength I didn't have. I tried to console her as if she would be the one fighting the virus. In no small way, she was going to. Our roles would be reversed soon enough. I felt my pulse racing.

Standing together, it was as if Carol and I were at the head of a trail that branched off in two different directions. One path was wide and dappled with sunlight under a perfect canopy of leaves reaching out from tall, straight trees evenly spaced along the trail. That trail was well worn with footprints and the echoes of travelers who had left their troubles behind. But it was not for us. Inviting as it may have been, it seemed to lead nowhere, bending into the undergrowth, to borrow a phrase from Robert Frost, and doubling back on itself endlessly.

The other path, narrow and strewn with brambles and debris as if in the aftermath of a storm, was dark and foreboding, its trees growing close as thieves. There were few signs along this path of previous travelers, yet it led by and by to a safe, well-lit clearing. Carol and I had to choose from these two paths—one simple, the other arduous. The path we chose would lead me through the darkest period in my life.

Somehow, on autopilot, I kept a light tone in my voice. I managed a smile. "Really?" I asked Carol, who was by now shivering and crying openly. "Looks like we'll have to beat it then, won't we?"

Chapter Two
The Night of My Life

Proverbs 16:16 tells us that it is better to receive wisdom than gold, and understanding rather than silver. I also believe that there is no knowledge greater than the knowledge of self, and fighting hepatitis C has instilled within me clarity of reason, judgment, and perspective. Pain can do that. While I may have boldly and perhaps blindly taken steps toward any given goal before my battle against hepatitis C, the disease taught me to tread lightly. It made me aware that each step leads to another, and you can retrace those steps to a better understanding of yourself. It forces you to examine where your steps may be headed, directed either by God, or misdirected without the guidance of His infinite wisdom. In this way I can recall what brought me to where I am today and it is helpful in understanding where my steps may lead me tomorrow.

I was born at Wright-Patterson Air Force Base in Dayton, Ohio, in 1969, the youngest of four children born to

Major Richard Prater and Barbara Fowler Prater. My oldest
sister, Ginny, was 12 when I was born, my brother Rich was
nine, and my sister Sandy was six. When I was four years
old, my father moved his family to Prattville, Alabama, on
the outskirts of Montgomery, the big city. Montgomery's
claim to fame was that it was once the capital of the confed-
eracy and it has since been in slow decline. For decades,
families have chosen instead to settle in Prattville. That's
where the Praters landed and that's where we would stay.

With my father's military career winding down, we
moved just once after arriving in Prattville to a home one
block away from our first home. Ginny, Rich, Sandy, and I
liked Prattville. We seemed to have as much stability as any
traditional household could offer: a domestic but indepen-
dent mother and a father I revered. He flew combat mis-
sions for 3 1/2 years over Vietnam in a C-130 Hercules and
at times took to the air for the Central Intelligence
Agency—a sworn soldier always vigilant in his duty. He dis-
played loyalty to his country overseas, while his wife was a
dedicated mother minding hearth and home.

But Barbara Fowler Prater has never been a weeping
willow. Born and raised in southeastern New York State,
she is as direct and opinionated as they come, and she rarely
hesitated if an opportunity arose to direct that Yankee point
of view at the major. When my father was assigned a year-
long tour of Seoul, Korea, my mother ruled the roost with
love, Methodist teachings, and a no-nonsense approach to
child rearing. We lived in what appeared to be one of the
most idyllic southern communities, though it was still reel-
ing from the senseless bigotry that had openly plagued the
nation and the south in particular for so long. My mother

and father taught all four of their children to measure a person by his character, not by the color of his skin. And my mother was peculiar about language, even the most innocuous southern terms; she counted the words *ain't*, *fixin'*, and *gonna* among the many swear words we were forbidden to use. I owe her my diction and gift of gab.

By the time my father returned to teach at the Air War College at Maxwell Air Force Base in Montgomery, my mother had acquired her teaching degree and our family seemed whole again.

I suppose I was too young to see what was ahead for them, though the signposts were clear. For all I knew I lived in a home where my parents doted on their children and on each other. Yet in the odd silences and the occasionally palpable tension that existed between them, we children began to see that all was not well. For as much love as my parents shared, my father's long absences had taken their toll and when together their personalities clashed too often, my mother's passion versus my father's military stoicism—fire and earth.

A series of separations began in 1976, which served only to delay the divorce in 1981. I remember the divorce as one of the most painful experiences of my life. The emotional turbulence I felt was matched only by the social stigma that was attached to children of divorce. To this day I have difficulty reconciling the act of divorce with my Christian beliefs. I know from personal experience the emotional hardship it visits upon families. There do exist valid reasons why two people joined together in holy matrimony might part, and no one plans on leaving a marriage while they are vowing before God to maintain a lifelong relationship. But nothing could make divorce easier for the children who are forced to stand by and watch as their young lives are shattered into domestic chaos.

My dad eventually moved away to Georgia and visited my mother and me on occasional weekends, my older brother and sisters having moved away to begin their own lives. With my father absent, I found solace in the open spaces of Prattville and in the friends I made in the neighborhood.

I became close with a boy named John McDaniel, whose parents owned a wonderful home that they kept open to their children's friends. John's father, Wayne, stepped in to fill some of the blank spaces left by my dad's absence. John and I stalked the neighborhood mourning doves with our Daisy BB and pellet guns, and Wayne included me in hunting and fishing trips. John and I grew to share a love of baseball, football, and girls.

The Night of My Life

Now, God has not blessed me with great stature or blinding speed. I was a cub playing for the Prattville High School Lions, standing 5 feet 6 inches tall and weighing 135 pounds. But what I lacked in physical dominance I made up for in enthusiasm. I watched most games from the sidelines as a second-string kicker and the third place running back, full of fire and eager to get my hands, or feet, on the ball. I got my wish during homecoming week, 1985.

We were scheduled to face Tuskegee High School, a team with more heart than talent, and we were almost assured a win. As an added bonus, I had managed to wrangle a date for the homecoming dance with a beauty named Terry Earnst.

During the week before the game, I suffered with a terrible sinus infection that caused some occasional nosebleeds. The team doctor attempted to treat me, but despite his best efforts the virus persisted. Later in the week I discovered blisters around my ankles and hips where clothing and padding were tightest. Yet, I had decided that nothing short of a commandment from the Lord Almighty was going to keep me from playing my first high school football game or going to the dance with an angel.

The mayor of Prattville pulled double duty as the game's public announcer. When he finally called my name it seemed to recall the resonant significance of Lou Gehrig's speech at Yankee Stadium when he announced that he felt like "the luckiest man on the face of the earth." That was exactly how I felt. My father was in the stands, back in town on one of his weekend visits, Terry was waiting for me after the game, and I even managed to kick a few extra points for the team.

After a shower, I went to the dance with Terry. I don't remember how well I hustled, but we danced in the clouds. I was set to wrap up my heady weekend with a round of golf with my dad the following morning, but I woke to a nasty surprise.

A Transfusion

Through the night I had developed more blisters, filled with blood and entirely frightening to my mother, who insisted I see a doctor. I had blood drawn at Autauga Medical Center. Dr. Kenny Nichols, on call for the weekend, laid out the bad news: I had somehow developed idiopathic thrombocytopenic purpura, or ITP, a disorder in which the body turns on itself. Instead of viruses, my spleen and immune system were attacking the platelets in my bloodstream, those microscopic lifesavers that slow blood flow in the event of an injury. Without them you can bleed to death from the smallest injury. My level of platelets was so low that my blood was roughly the consistency of water. "You may be bleeding in your brain right now," Dr. Nichols said, "and there's nothing I can do to stop it. So you're going two rooms down and you're not going to move."

I was 16 years old, not nearly old enough, I believed, for the Lord to call me home, especially after the night of my life. Numb with apprehension, I did what I was told and no one in the family questioned the need for or the safety of a platelet transfusion. I was given two transfusions equaling 20 pints of blood. I can say with near certainty that this was where the battle lines were drawn for the fight of my life.

Screening blood in 1985 was not a common practice, and because the medical community was unfamiliar with hepatitis C at the time, there is no guarantee they would have discovered it in the blood supply that gave me life-saving platelets. The disease didn't even have a name until 1992. It was simply known as Unknown Hepatitis A and B. Nearly 10% of all cases of Hepatitis C have been shown to be caused by blood transfusions. Before 1990, donated blood was not tested for hepatitis C. Since 1993, the risk of getting hepatitis C from a blood transfusion has been insignificant.

Looking back, I recognize that football game as a pivotal point in my life, when I took a path that would affect me in years to come. Though I would not realize it until years later, this path would lead me through pain and revelation, it would close some doors and open others, and it would force me to recognize the true power of faith and prayer.

While in the hospital undergoing the transfusion, doctors asked me if I'd recently been hit in the head or body. I recall thinking that it was a strange question. The answer, however, was simple. As a place kicker I avoided the harsh practices my teammates experienced and during games I practically went untouched. I was later told that if I had been hit hard enough, I would have likely died on the field.

The workings of the Lord's plan for each of us is wonderfully puzzling, none more so than in the wildly interconnected strands of a man's purpose.

The Storm of a Lifetime

In Alabama, where the gridiron is practically a church and football a religion, I was in love with the weather. I became absorbed in my father's books on meteorology and there was no shortage of real world research to be had. All I had to do was look out my window.

There is an old saying that March comes in like a lion and goes out like a lamb. The lion of March would run away with its tail between its legs if it ever had to tangle with the severe thunderstorms and tornadoes that spring and summer bring to Alabama.

At the ABC affiliate in Birmingham in April 1998, I was reporting on the usual round of spring's stormy weather. By then I was already preparing my audience for the steamy temperatures on the way in a matter of weeks. I had, I suppose, discounted the rest of spring, assuming that its relatively stable pattern would continue until summer. I could not have been more wrong.

Part of my fascination with weather is the way that so many random conditions have to come together in just the right way to produce such spectacular events. It's the reason why forecasts can be entirely off the mark. Some storms build on the horizon without warning, or the warning itself is of a harmless squall, and then it strikes with torrential rains or turns the world white with snow and ice. Every meteorologist has a story like this, and he or she fears leaving the job after work and to be pelted with snowballs by an angry mob that was duped into thinking no storm would come.

But on this April day the computer models were painting a chilling picture. The atmosphere was hot and humid, and a strong jet stream was moving over the state. The Severe Storms Forecast Center had put much of central Alabama under a high risk for major storms and damaging tornadoes, and by 5 P.M. on April 8 my worst fears were confirmed. Nine counties were under a tornado warning, and radar scans were showing a deadly rotating super-cell thunderstorm heading in our direction.

Throughout the evening as our team of forecasters kept our audience abreast of storm activity, I could barely tear myself away from the radar screen. Storm spotters squawked crackling messages across Hamm radio channels. A retired National Weather Service sharpshooter named J.B. Elliot came in to help us track the skies. Dumbfounded by what I was seeing, I turned to J.B. "My God, it's on the ground," I said. It was a hunch. Radar can't really tell you if a tornado has touched down; you need visual confirmation. But eight minutes later the Hamm radio operators began screaming. "We've got damage, significant damage!" That was our cue. We had been on the air for hours now, but our level of intensity blew through the roof as we went on air with an urgent warning. "This tornado is on the ground, take cover immediately. This is a tornado emergency; those in the track of this storm must take cover. Immediately!"

The tornado was an F-5, classified as the most dangerous of all whip-cracking weather monsters. It measured three-quarters of a mile in diameter and anything that stood in its way was being eaten alive. As the twister swept toward downtown Birmingham, small communities west of the city were being wiped clean.

Pratt City, a town on the western edge of Birmingham, was next. The twister came on relentlessly, heralding its arrival with black skies and the roar of a massive train. This spinning column of death roared head on into Pratt City, which took heavy damage and loss of life, but after raining blows upon this innocent community the tornado suddenly lifted and stayed airborne, sparing Birmingham the same fate. Thirty-four souls went to Jesus that night, and some towns remain scarred to this day.

The storm had exacted a heavy emotional toll on the region as well. No one had expected such severe conditions. I was glad to have been able to raise an alarm, but the decisions our team made that night continued to haunt me for months. Could we have gotten the warnings on the air sooner? Could we have been more precise?

It wasn't until June of that year that I realized how valuable that urgent information really had been for many people who had tuned in to our station for storm updates. I was shopping for a pair of sunglasses on my birthday in a local Wal-Mart when a man cautiously limped into my peripheral vision. I was prepared to turn to him and smile, quite used to being approached in this manner by people on the street who regularly said hello. His voice was gentle and he said something I won't ever forget. "You know you saved my life." I looked up. The man was accompanied by his wife, and he was leaning heavily on crutches. He had obviously been injured. He said, "We watched you on the night of April 8th, and it was just the way you said something with such urgency that I grabbed my wife's arm and dove into our hallway. Our house exploded seconds later. I'm just now getting out of the hospital, but my wife and I are alive because of you. Thank you for what you did, Mark."

I was stunned and I managed to utter a few words before staggering back to my van where Carol and our children waited. I sat there while Carol looked at me intently. "What's the matter?" she asked. I didn't say a word as a tear ran down my face. For months I'd put my emotions aside, subconsciously paving over the ruts and holes the night of the storm had left in its wake. It had taken that long for me to finally come to terms with it.

I'd labored that night to warn as many people as possible of the clear and present danger of the fatal storm, but when you're in the television studio number of people in the viewing audience becomes abstract—it is virtually impossible to imagine yourself speaking simultaneously to a million people. I realized that when you can see, talk to, and touch the people you help during a disaster, all of your efforts become validated. It hits you like a mallet on a steel anvil.

What really strikes me, however, is the resilience of the battle-weary people who survive that kind of attack from above. *It is God's will*, many of them say while surveying the debris that was once their home, or cradling broken family heirlooms, or mourning lost loved ones. Anger and sadness linger for only so long before survivors raise their chins and set to work rebuilding. I realize there is great lesson to be learned here. Man is not the master of his own fate. Though a catastrophic event may rob you of everything that is dear to you, your home, your possessions, your health, God has given you strength to survive and to rebuild. It is the most valuable lesson I ever learned, one that would serve me well in the fight against a silent killer.

Chapter Three
Facing the Storm

When I was diagnosed with hepatitis C, I felt that it was not a socially acceptable disease. I remember thinking, "Hepatitis C. Is that some kind of sexually-transmitted disease? It's in the same neighborhood, isn't it?" There has been a kind of stigma associated with hepatitis C, probably because the easiest identifiable cause in the past was intravenous drug use. We have since learned that the hepatitis C virus (HCV) can be passed by many possible sources of contact with infected blood—intravenous drug use, yes, but also transfusions, dialysis, being born to an infected mother, exposure in a health-care environment, even sharing a razor or toothbrush. The stigma was something to overcome. A disease like cancer, for example, allows for a thousand morale-building organized efforts to help its victims. Somehow to me cancer seemed like a more "acceptable" thing to have, maybe because cancer is not contagious. I had to get over that.

One of the first emotions I felt after the shock of discovery was fear. I didn't understand the disease. I was afraid that this unknown predator was stalking healthy cells in my body, and that because it is communicable I was posing a danger to those closest to me. What did acquiring hepatitis C mean for my family? I asked my physician. Could Carol have already been infected? What was the risk to my children? To my great relief I was told that hepatitis C is not sexually transmitted unless there has been a transmission of blood. And it is not passed on to children except through the mother during delivery.

This was a great relief, but it failed to erase my instinctual revulsion at having the disease. And I knew that if I was disgusted, others might be as well. The response to most victims of catastrophic, non-contagious diseases is typically sympathetic, and rightly so. But if you say you have hepatitis C the immediate response may be different. My favorite actor Denzel Washington gave a perfect example of this type of reaction in the movie *Philadelphia*. When Tom Hanks' character tells Denzel's character that he has AIDS, Denzel's body language is suddenly self-protective, as if Hanks had just stepped out of a pile of radioactive garbage. That's generally how I felt when I was diagnosed, and that's what I think other people feel; they don't want to discuss it. You wonder if people are going to judge you.

I was afraid of being judged, but fortunately I had a supportive group of family and friends. The people who make up this inner circle are as critical to healing as prayer and medicine. The body cannot survive without the soul, and during the long road back to recovery the people who stay with you, pray with you, lift your spirits, and remind you that life continues beyond the stormy skies under which you have stood for so long—these people are the ones you thank God for putting in your life. I had no idea how the news of my contracting hepatitis C would be received by my friends or by the public. Would they judge me or would they support me?

The time had come for me to announce my condition to the people who let me gab all morning on television. Garry Kelly, the news director, sat stock still as I sat in his office and described what was in store for me and how it would affect his news operation. It's a hard thing to tell your boss that you may be absent for long periods of time over the next six months. In my worst nightmares, Garry would have shrugged his shoulders and said, "Sorry, kid. I need people who work for me to be at work, not at home throwing up in their bunny slippers. But good luck. By the way, do you know any meteorologists looking for a job?" True to form, however, Garry let me have my say and replied, "You do whatever you've got to do. We're here for you and you'll always have any support you need. Take off as much time as you want." I would have hugged him, but Garry's gruff expression reminded me that I was in no shape to take any retaliatory punishment.

I got a similar response from Garry's boss, Roy Clem, the station's general manager. It was a huge relief to know that my position at work was secure. I prayed and thanked God for putting such good Christian men in my path.

Telling Our Children

But as nerve-wracking as this experience was, I remembered how anxious I had been to include my own family in the discovery. Carol knew, of course, but we'd kept the children in the dark for as long as possible, preferring to see how things would have to be done.

I chose to speak first to my oldest son, Cole. Before my treatments began Carol and I sat down with him to deliver the news. I'd practiced what I was going to say, and it had seemed deliberate and reasonable, designed to lessen the blow that I was sure he'd feel, knowing him as I did. Of course it came out of my mouth less organized, shuffled into tactless delivery by my jostling emotions.

"Son, Daddy's sick!" I said. Cole nodded.

"Yes sir," he replied.

"I've got a disease called hepatitis C and I'm very sick right now," I continued, barreling through it. "But, Cole, I'm going to battle it with medicine and chemotherapy and beat this virus."

He just sat and said, "Yes sir" in agreement. To this day I don't know what he was really thinking at the time, but he showed a great interest in hearing what I had to say with a minimum of demonstrative emotion. I knew better. Cole is an emotional kid with a heart so big it shines through in everything he does. God truly blessed me and Carol with that child. He is even-keeled and compassionate well beyond his years, and along with that compassion is a sensitivity that is his blessing and his curse. We worried that he would be deeply wounded. After we'd had our talk Cole calmly retreated upstairs to his room, and Carol and I exchanged relieved glances. "That went well," I said.

I found out later that he was more curious than he'd let on. He approached Carol while I was away and gently but pointedly asked her, "Mom, is this going to kill Daddy?"

Carol reassured him. "No, son, the disease is not going to kill him if he gets treatments. But the treatments are extremely serious and will make him very sick."

"Well, how did he get this?" my boy asked her.

"Through a blood transfusion years ago," Carol answered. He wanted to know if the family had been exposed to hepatitis C (by some miracle for which I thank Almighty God, they had not) and seemed concerned that I was going to be subjected to weekly injections. He'd been mulling over everything.

There was an unpleasant stretch of weeks before my scheduled chemotherapy when the virus was raging through my blood and it had begun to affect my mood. I was short with the people I love and in the face of imminent pain I let my emotions get the best of me. My fuse was so short that I'd explode over the simplest of ordinary children's transgressions. I didn't even realize it was happening, but once Carol pointed it out we developed a code word that she would mention when she saw me become aggressive with the children. I don't recall what the word was, but the memory of my children crying as a result of my verbal abuse is something that will haunt me for as long as I draw breath.

Of all the children, Cole was the one old enough to openly question my erratic behavior. He asked Carol when she went to tuck him in one night, "Momma, why is Daddy so mad at me?" Carol said, "Son, he's not. He's sick right now and this disease is what makes him this way. He doesn't mean it and he still loves you so much. He's hurting all of the time and facing a lot ahead. He cares for you more than he can possibly say. This is just a bad week."

Cole's stoicism failed him this time, and he reached out

and held Carol close to him, tears streaking his anguished face. "I'm trying so hard to be strong for him. I hate this disease. I HATE this disease! I want my Daddy back!" Ever the rock, Carol reassured him that we were going to fight the disease and win. "But we've got to fight through problems that come with it," she said. "Just know your Daddy absolutely adores you and he will get better. We'll have him back when he's won!"

Knowing how difficult it had been for Cole, I knew I could count on my siblings to absorb the blow with hope and encouragement. Sandy, my closest sister in age, and her husband Andy, whom I consider a second brother, vowed to be supportive through the treatments, often using humor and picking at me to keep me honest. They kept their promise. My oldest sister Virginia, who we call Ginny, was also dedicated to comforting me with many phone calls.

My mother and father took it hard, but like my siblings they pledged their support and simply declared that I would have to stand up and beat it. Hepatitis C was going to be no match for the Praters. I've been so blessed to have two brothers and two sisters who have never wavered in their love for me. Like anyone else, my family has its share of problems and disagreements. Families who never disagree only live in the minds of sitcom writers. But the strength of familial love God has put into the hearts of the Praters is unrelenting.

My siblings always took care to keep me grounded as I grew in my career. They took pains to remind me that I'd worn diapers and cried for attention long before anyone asked me for an autograph. I'd always be their little brother, though they took pride in any accomplishment I achieved, as I did in theirs. Despite our parents' separation, that's one thing both of them generously instilled in all of us: our love for one another. As we age, succeed, struggle, and grow, we get closer every year.

When I told them what was happening and what was ahead for me, they were stunned, but remained strong. I needed that. I did not need crippling pity or abject sorrow. I was sturdy on the outside, but my stomach was turning somersaults. I had to be strong and prove I was ready for whatever came my way, but they knew me too well. I couldn't hide it from them. Still, they told me how proud they were of how I was facing this disease. They knew that I would do my best to stand tall against the strongest winds.

I turned back to breaking the news to the rest of my children. Our girls, Madison and Trinity, were too young to fully understand the impact the news would have on our family, but in a way that was a relief. I was burdened enough by the illness and by having to put so much on Carol's shoulders right from the start.

Carol

My respect for Carol is immeasurable. Her strength through the ordeal kept me going when all else seemed designed to bring me to an end. I am truly blessed to have found her, because when we first met I wasn't looking for love.

The first lesson she ever taught me is that love is like a swinging door: it hits you square on the nose when you just aren't paying attention. I met Carol Willis in 1993. We must have run into each other a thousand times between playing volleyball at church and attending worship. At the time, I was admittedly a rather self-involved person. I was working at the NBC affiliate in Montgomery, Alabama, reporting three days a week on the street, and anchoring weather on the weekends. This was my dream come true. I put in 50 to 70 hours a week because that's what the job required, which left me just enough time to raise heck as a single man.

I regularly took advantage of the attention I received as a "famous" television personality. If an attractive single woman approached wanting an autograph, I could turn that into a date, and I did that often enough to make commitment to any one of them a distant consideration.

Then Carol Willis came into my life. I never noticed her until one day after a volleyball game at church I saw one of my friends talking to this delicate brunette. I crossed the gym to strike up a conversation with them both. You always learn a little more about the nature of women by listening to them talk to each other. I was in for a great lesson. They were discussing Carol's divorce. The topic stopped me in my tracks so fast I left skid marks on the gym floor. I knew nothing about Carol and I certainly didn't want to hear about her marital problems. A newly divorced woman was as appealing to me as a string of garlic is to a vampire. I hissed and bared my fangs and concocted some excuse to beat a hasty retreat to my coffin.

I almost made a clean getaway when my friend caught up to me and threw out the suggestion that I join them for a bite to eat. I had to weigh this. I wasn't due to work until the following evening, I was hungry, and the establishment was practically within walking distance. So I said yes.

At the restaurant, Carol and I fell into an easy rhythm, chatting amiably. I noticed with increasing appreciation her long, black, curly hair and I learned that her divorce was a painful, necessary thing—not casual at all. My attention was cleanly diverted, however, when an attractive acquaintance of mine dropped by the table. Presumably to leave our seating arrangements intact, she sat right down on my lap. We politely included her in our conversation, though she was blocking my view of Carol. That's when I felt a searing pain on my left shin, the result of some deft footwork on Carol's part.

"Oh," she said, "I'm sorry about that. Didn't know your leg was under there." A little jealousy goes a long way. Carol was looking even better to me after I knew she was interested.

The next evening, we grabbed something to eat after my evening broadcast. Carol spoke openly about her failed marriage and her plans for the immediate future. I got a glimpse of a strong woman with strong Christian beliefs and from that moment on, I believe I was hooked. I reached out to her again on the following day and a nagging voice from the old Mark Prater rang in my head. "Have you lost your mind? Three days in a row?" But I knew better. First Corinthians 13:11 says, "When I was a child, I talked like a child, I thought like a child, I reasoned like a child. When I became a man, I put childish ways behind me" (NIV). It can be broadly interpreted, yet that passage can easily refer to love, and in the connection that was quickly forming between Carol and me I put away the selfish notions that had held sway over my juvenile dating habits. I developed a deep respect for Carol that was growing into something far greater.

Four months after that encounter in the church gym I was ready to accept a new way of life. Ready to put away childish things. It was the smartest decision I have ever made.

We were married on June 25th, 1994. We have been blessed with four children and have grown ever closer as a family.

Since hepatitis C came to disrupt my family and my home, I came to rely on Carol for far more than companionship. She became my strongest advocate and my spiritual rock.

Chapter Four
Beginning Treatment

In the beginning, Carol and I had more questions than answers about the disease. As important as it is to understand your illness, medical jargon sometimes stands in the way. From the very beginning it is critically important to establish an open dialogue with your physician. It is equally important to feel comfortable enough to stop him or her when you may not understand something about your medical options and ask to be taken through the process step by step. Carol and I were both forced to press our doctors for clear and simple answers, and as a result we gleaned some critical details from the overwhelming tide of information.

We learned that the liver is the unsung hero of the human body. It regulates the body's storage of nutrients such as glucose, vitamins, and minerals, it transforms food into energy, and it is the heavyweight champion of purification, transformation, and clearance of waste products, drugs, and toxins. A damaged liver can turn the body into a walking landfill. The liver also produces most of the proteins responsible for blood clotting and plays an important role in hormonal balance. A person cannot live without a liver.

What Is Hepatitis C?

Hepatitis C is a virus that attacks the liver. It is virtually undetectable in its early stages. The virus can spend years slowly attacking your liver, while you notice only flu-like symptoms that come and go. Hepatitis C is very difficult for the immune system to defeat, because it mutates rapidly and outmaneuvers the immune system. It lurks in the blood for years undetected, because the early symptoms are often very mild. The most common symptom, beginning sometimes years after the infection, is fatigue. Other symptoms include mild fever, muscle and joint aches, nausea, vomiting, appetite loss, abdominal pain, and sometimes diarrhea.

After years of ongoing, slow damage by the hepatitis C virus, the liver becomes badly damaged. The virus can cause the liver to form scars, which prevent blood from flowing freely through the organ. The later stages of the virus lead to cirrhosis and liver failure, with symptoms including jaundice, abdominal swelling due to water retention, and coma. Hepatitis C can lead to death. There is no vaccine for hepatitis C at present. However, due to the virus' slow progress, people with hepatitis C can have long life expectancies and can even recover completely, with treatment.

Hepatitis C is the liver's greatest enemy; it is the leading cause of liver transplants. The disease targets nearly 10,000 American victims each year. More than 4 million Americans are already in its sights, a figure that is expected to increase fourfold over the next decade. Perhaps the most insidious aspect of this biological assassin is that it convinces the victim that it doesn't exist; up to 80 percent of people infected with hepatitis C are unaware of its presence.

Determining the Damage

My doctor's first task was to confirm the extent of the damage already done to my liver, the primary target for hepatitis C. He needed a physical sample of the liver via a biopsy. It was an unpleasant experience, and when I say "unpleasant," I'm being kind. A doctor who specializes in these kinds of procedures inserted a rather large needle into my liver. Attached to it was a trigger that the doctor would pull to get a proper sample. I felt the metal shaft sink into my body and I let out a low grunt as the needle seemed to meet with resistance in the liver itself. The doctor pushed the needle deeper and I wanted nothing more than to get it out. I was Mark Prater, the human shish kabob. Then I heard the click of the trigger as the doctor took his sample—his pound of flesh, if you will—and he extracted the needle. The doctor and nurses covered the entry point with gauze and pushed hard to apply pressure, I assume to help stem blood flow. I was sore for days afterward, but we weren't finished yet.

To get a complete picture of the damage doctors also needed an ultrasound of my liver. I was already more than a little afraid, though I refused to let it show; this reaction is a holdover from my childhood when I was quick to put on a brave front when faced with emotional turmoil. I wanted to be strong for my family, but as I turned to look at the ultrasound monitor I began searching for dark spots that could mean I had developed tumors, possibly cancerous. This is the path that advanced hepatitis C can take. My grandfather, Bernie Prater, died of pancreatic cancer. My mom's dad, Tazwell Fowler, died of lung cancer. Sadly, the list goes on and on through too many branches of the family tree. I prayed that my odds were better than those of my unfortunate relatives.

Upon close examination, doctors assured me that the dark spots they saw were due to a damaged liver, but no tumors were present. The damage, however, was significant, in the way that an alcoholic's liver would have been damaged. During the biopsy the needle did not pass smoothly through my liver because extensive scar tissue had formed and had presented the needle with barriers that the assistant punched through to get the sample. I had not developed cirrhosis yet, but I was moving toward it and it was imperative that we stop the progress of the disease.

The Treatment Plan

To battle the disease, our doctors armed us with an effective concoction of medicine: pegylated interferon, a protein to boost my immune system, and ribavirin, a drug that prevents the hepatitis C virus from multiplying. Interferon is a naturally occurring substance produced in the body when we have the flu or a viral illness. It is a bear of a substance and is responsible for the ravages of depression, anxiety, and flu-like symptoms that accompany hepatitis C therapy (these symptoms are created because the interferon is fighting the virus). We were told that once a week for approximately six months I would inject Peg-Intron (interferon) through the fat of the arm, the inside thigh, or one inch above my navel. To control swelling at the injection point I could use cortisone. I would also be taking Rebetol, ribavirin in pill form, twice daily. As of the printing of this book, the National Institutes of Health recognizes that the highest response rates in the treatment of chronic hepatitis C have been achieved with combination therapy with ribavirin and pegylated alpha interferons.

Hepatitis C is comprised of five genotypes, three of which are generally found in the United States. By far the most common is genotype one, the most difficult and resistant type to treat. This genotype, which is present in 75 to 80% of all hepatitis C patients in the United States, requires a full year of therapy. The good news was that I had been diagnosed with genotype two, for which the response rate is higher and the length of treatment shorter. Still, I was in for a long, hard ride.

In some ways treatment for hepatitis C is similar to chemotherapy for cancer. Interferon is used in much higher doses in cancer-related therapy, but the side effects are remarkably alike. The therapy can lower blood counts; it can affect your thyroid and other organs that are susceptible to immune mediated injury. Liver experts don't even seem to know how ribavirin works, but it seems to make interferon work better. The major problem with ribavirin is that in a subset of people it can cause red blood cells to break up in the bloodstream, a process called hemolytic anemia. That lowers blood counts and increases your fatigue. Blessed again, that never became a factor for me.

Interferon causes anxiety and irritability, so it poses a special problem for people with underlying problems, high stress jobs, or people like me who are required to be perpetually polite. I don't have the luxury to blow off steam at will. Though a patient may be able to keep emotional outbursts under control for a matter of weeks during the initial treatments, it would require a person of perfectly divine patience to remain civil for six months to a year. There is no one perfect but Jesus, and I'm sure not Him.

Avoiding the Dangers

I was told to watch for signs of depression, to be alert to numbness, and to take note of my temperature, which required medical attention if above 102 degrees. I was warned to cover cuts with bandages and not to share razors or toothbrushes. I was told there was a danger of sexual dysfunction. I was to pay special attention to my eyes because the medicines occasionally had an effect on the retina. In addition to all of these potential dangers, having hepatitis C predisposes you to hepatitis A & B, so I needed to be vaccinated against both. I was told that the first six weeks of treatment would be like experiencing a bad flu, with possible vomiting and diarrhea, and that I should have plenty of over-the-counter cold remedies and pain relievers on hand. Doctors told me without the slightest hint of irony that I should try to go on as normal. I was told to take frequent naps and stay positive.

It was a lot to digest all at once. Yet of all the advice, staying positive would present the greatest challenge. During this time I was being battered by my emotions, the worst of which was the sense of frustration that I was not in control of my own body. It is the most disconcerting feeling I could have imagined, as if strings were attached to my hands and feet and the disease was orchestrating my every move. I tried to do anything to fill my time in a way that I felt I could control, all the while wondering how I would put my life on hold for six months while I fought against the unwelcome visitor in my veins.

I had other questions, too. Should we shield the children from my treatments, which I assumed would be too difficult to watch? Would I be able to continue at work, delivering the weather day in and day out as a bright and sunny anchor? More importantly, would I still be able to lead my family and be a strong father to my children? No doctor could provide those answers. It brought to mind Proverbs 19:21, which reads, "Many are the plans in a man's heart, but it is the LORD's purpose that prevails" (NIV). Yet I was comforted again by the Word of God. Romans 8:28 reads, "In all things God works for the good of those who love him" (NIV). There was a design in what was happening and what was to come. I had to trust God to see me through to His ultimate purpose. I learned during this time how the Bible and its Scriptures could give me hope, to teach me to pray, and to show me how to believe in miracles. Carol and I felt we were going to need a miracle. Two would have been better.

I decided right at the beginning that no one but my wife was going to put that little needle in my arm. I could not have done it myself, and by the time the interferon began to take its toll I was glad I hadn't attempted to take on the responsibility. Carol at once became my nurse, ready and able around the clock to do what had to be done.

We were meticulous about our preparation for my very first treatment. We checked and rechecked the needle, making sure we were drawing the saline from the correct vial and mixing it with a powdered form of interferon from another. We shook the mixture until it turned a milky white color. The medicines were precious and we'd had to wait for them for several weeks. Evidently, as it was explained to us, the drug companies will not deliver these meds to you until your name comes up on a list that must be a mile long, owing to the enormous number of people being treated for hep C nationally. To add to our misery, we were told our names wouldn't come up until the company could guarantee enough meds for me to finish my six months of treatments. We were resigned to this delay. Carol and I waited, and in August 2002, our time had come.

A Prayerful Beginning

The disease had struck first, and now it was our turn to strike back with the first of many injections. We got comfortable in our living room and Carol swabbed the triceps of my left arm with an alcohol-soaked pad of cotton. We had been instructed to alternate arms each week to avoid a deterioration of the skin and muscle. Carol held the needle poised when I stopped her, as if to say, "I'm not ready. There has been a mistake and I'm actually perfectly healthy. Take that poison away!" In fact, I was physically ready, but my spirit needed reassurance. Carol watched me carefully.

Earlier in the day we discussed how we were going to approach the treatments. We were going to forge ahead and follow the doctor's orders, meet hepatitis C head on and bolster our spirits with faith. Matthew 17:20 says, "If ye have faith as a grain of mustard seed, ye shall say unto this mountain, Remove hence to yonder place; and it shall remove: and nothing shall be impossible unto you." Carol and I were desperately in need of a sense of security, a modicum of peace that had been stolen along with my health. "Let's turn this over to God and allow Him to be the Great Physician," I told her. "Let's pray."

We bowed our heads and our prayer came pouring out in a flood of emotion.

> *Dear heavenly Father, we both come to You in prayer, believing that You know our very souls, God, knowing that we are much in need of Your loving grace. Lord of mercy, we ask that You be our magnificent healer. We turn this over to You. Father, we know it will be difficult to stay the course, but with Your strength and guidance we will beat this disease. Please comfort our hearts, our minds, and those of our family during this time. We come to You with total and complete faith that You will fulfill Your promise to always be there for us if only we ask.*
>
> *Dear Lord, we ask for Your eternal vigilance tonight and throughout this entire treatment. We cannot know what lies ahead, but we'll follow You and keep our faith strong. Help us with our fears and our doubts. Let us know that You are here with us. Please God, as I may falter, shelter Carol and our children in Your loving embrace while we begin the battle for my health tonight.*
>
> *God, thank You for everything that You have given us. All of the blessings—our*

family, our faith, and our health. Thank
You, God, for allowing me to fight this bat-
tle. Show me how it will make me a better
father, husband, and servant to You, Lord.
Thank You, God for loving us so uncondi-
tionally. I now start this journey to serve
You. All of these things we pray in Jesus
Christ, our Lord and Savior. Amen.

From that moment, I turned my fears and doubts over to
God. This is not to say that I no longer had fears or doubts,
but I trusted Him in all things great and small. I was ready
to accept any adversity He or the world placed in front of
me. I realized that there were lessons to be had along this
journey. I could not have known what those lessons were
going to be, or how I would apply them in my own life, but
I was open to His way, which is why I thanked Him even
for the blessing of the disease. It sounds like a contradiction.
Blessing of the disease. But there is no joy without sadness,
no pleasure without pain. A man cannot know peace unless
he has experienced chaos, and by facing the depths of hell,
he discovers the greatness of heaven. God was showing
Carol and me and our children His capacity for love, and
perhaps testing our faith. We were determined not to fail.

I looked into Carol's eyes, smiled and said, "Let's do it."
As the tears welled up in her eyes and began to run down
her cheeks, she sniffed and let out a sad little laugh and
said, "I don't know if I can do this." I knew she could.
She'd given birth to our children, each one of them perfect.
Jabbing me with needles was going to be unpleasant, I reasoned, but comparatively speaking, far easier than giving

birth! I told her that we stood the best chance of success together. I remember her saying, "I don't want to be the one to make you sick. When I put this in you, it's me that's making you sick. Plus, I'm scared." I remained upbeat and said, "We'll be okay, babe. We'll be okay! Let's do this and see what happens next!"

I became a one-man pep squad as she prepared the injection. Her hands were shaking. "Okay," she said, "are you ready?" I turned my head and stared at the wall and everything inside of me was screaming, *No, no I'm not ready and if I thought about it long enough, I never would be.* But it was time. I lied. "I'm ready."

My brother Rich is a registered nurse and he told Carol that the best way to get the feel for administering injections is to practice on an orange. As a result, there were plenty of pierced pieces of fruit in the kitchen, but Carol went through the motions like a pro, aided by a specific set of directions that had accompanied the medicine. At the time, we were required to manually mix the powdered form of Peg-Intron with sterile water using vials and syringes and careful measurements. This is no longer necessary, as drug companies have designed more sophisticated methods of preparation. But at the time, the directions read like a medical manual: "Carefully remove the cap from one of your syringes. Draw back on the plunger to get 0.7 ml of air. Insert this needle into your sterile water. Holding the sterile water upright with one hand while holding the syringe with the other hand, slowly draw back on the plunger while watching for the formation of bubbles. If a bubble appears, push the water back into the vial and slowly pull back again. Repeat this process until you draw up only 0.7 ml of water. Inject the syringe through the plastic hub of the Peg-Intron vial. Prepare the injection site..." It went on like this for some time. Carol became familiar with the ritual and prepared the drugs. She pinched my arm, and then I felt a slight pressure in my triceps just above my elbow as the syringe went in under the skin. The concoction burned a little going into my arm, but the sensation was nothing like the excruciating pain and bleeding for which I had prepared myself. I felt foolish. What had all the fuss been about? Carol sniffed and said, "Okay, that's it, sweetie! We're done." She was great. We were over the first big hurdle and I was feeling fine. "Thank you," I said, and leaned over to kiss her. "I love you."

We wondered if we'd gone into this treatment with more anxiety than was warranted. Had we overreacted? It seemed so. For more than an hour I was feeling great. Same for the second hour and into the third. What could I have possibly been so concerned about? With a sense of well being I went to bed, not as steady as I normally am, but I knew that my nerves were working overtime and for the moment I discounted the gently rolling waves under my feet. I prayed to God and thanked Him for making the beginning of this journey so effortless, and for helping Carol through it all. I felt reassured. "You know what?" I asked myself. "I can do this. Thank You, God. Thank You so very much. I love You, Lord." With a prayer on my lips, I fell into a deep sleep.

The next morning, my reassurance was gone. I wondered if I hadn't been prescribed battery acid, because it felt like someone had pumped me full of it. I woke up with a fever of 101.5 and in the midst of the pain I remembered I was scheduled for another dose of Rebetol—twice a day while I was taking the interferon. I swallowed as much Advil as I could manage. By midday I was aggressively throwing up and I could swear someone had struck a church bell in my head. Pain relievers eased my discomfort and allowed me to rest for a time, but eventually the flu-like symptoms would return with a vengeance. I buried myself under a mountain of blankets, shivering, while Carol kept a steady supply of cold rags pressed to my overheated forehead.

Over the course of the next several days, I went to my knees often, and not just to pray. My spine and joints felt like they were being squeezed in a vise. Things came out of me that I never knew existed. I half expected to find long lost childhood toys, and my condition was serious enough that Carol decided to pack me in the car and drive me back to the doctor's office for an explanation.

Side Effects

As much as we thought we knew what to expect, I was not really prepared for the side effects. I was even less prepared for the response we received from the doctor who initially treated me. While we explained the difficulties I was having, he appeared aloof and cemented that impression over the course of the next several minutes. "Well, I don't understand," he said, his arms crossed in a pose a scientist might adopt while examining an exotic virus. "You should have some discomfort, but I've never heard of anything this severe." He had not apparently heard from other patients, who warned us that the treatment would dwarf the actual disease in the pain and emotional torment department. But he followed this statement with a complete contradiction:

"I've put a few doctors on this and they had to quit taking the treatment," he said. I asked him why. "They couldn't handle it." That's when Carol and I made a choice to find someone who understood what I was going through and would comprehensively be able to prepare me and my family for what was to come. I felt that I was being correctly treated for hepatitis C, but I felt the emotional damage was being ignored. Carol and I decided that one could not be effectively treated without the other.

Divine providence intervened. At the time I was first undergoing treatments, one of the station's anchors, Brenda Ladun, as classy and beautiful a woman as they come, had just completed chemotherapy for her breast cancer. While I witnessed her struggle with the potentially deadly illness, I had admired her courage and her strong sense of determination, thoroughly grounded in her faith in God. Brenda became a dynamo of breast cancer education and awareness. She went to every fundraiser, marched in every march, and spoke at every function she could manage in her hectic schedule to make people aware of breast cancer as a disease to defeat.

She'd done a promotional television spot for a fundraiser and had appeared with a woman named Ashley Watkins, who was an attorney and, as I found out, a hepatitis C survivor. I called Ashley out of the blue and over time I discovered a warm and helpful friend. Throughout the course of my treatments I called her with questions about my condition, or simply to talk to someone with answers. She never let me down, and I have to thank her for putting me in touch with Dr. Mike Fallon, a liver specialist at the University of Alabama at Birmingham Medical Center.

Dr. Fallon and I clicked immediately. I prefer that people say what they mean and say it up front. Mike had my records, was aware of my treatment and my reaction to the interferon, but he was not going to hold my hand and promise me that the treatments were going to be any less miserable under his care. "You're likely to be irritable," he said. "You may have trouble at work and feel like garbage when you have to get up at 4 o'clock in the morning to tell people about the weather. You're not going to be able to run around town and do charity events like you used to. You're going to lose your hair. You're going to be spending a lot more time with doctors than you want to. Probably it's going to get worse and worse as you go along. And you'll end up having to apologize to your wife for the next ten years."

I hated to hear it, but it was better to hear the truth. On any given day we struggle with what we choose to believe. Some days the devil makes a better case with his lies. But the truth from this doctor helped quiet the whispers of doubt and fear in my head; it helped strengthen my faith, which had taken a beating early in the journey. I stopped wondering whether I was overreacting to the pain. I wasn't. The truth made shadows out of the once-concrete conviction in the first week of treatment that I would be better off dead. I had been mortally afraid and that fear spoke to me as plainly as I ever spoke to anyone in my life. From the depths of my mind I heard it begging, "Oh, Carol...please go into the closet and get out the gun. Just put it to my forehead and kill me. Then shoot me in my spine to make it quit hurting. Then shoot me in my knees and ankles. I'm afraid they'll still hurt after I'm dead. Baby, please...please just kill me."

I earnestly tried to put that voice behind me once I knew what to expect. I thank God for putting Dr. Fallon in our path.

Together we adjusted my therapy so that I would take my interferon on Fridays instead of the middle of the week. That meant my weekend would be ruined, but I could usually count on being able to go to work on Mondays. I cut back on my speaking tours and charity events. I took regular pain medication as needed and talked to doctors about anti-depressants. I was able to refocus on the support my family was giving me. I was able to prepare myself for letting the public in on my secret.

Chapter Five
The Show Goes On

Ideveloped a regular routine to maintain a semblance of order in my life. Typically I would wake up at 4 A.M. I'd grab a peanut butter sandwich, take one Lortab, an Advil, supplements, and vitamins, and I'd head to the television station for the morning broadcast. If I made it through an entire shift, I would return home at about 9 A.M. That's when I'd take ribavirin and another dose of Advil for my joint and muscle pain. I would lie down, exhausted, and nap for about an hour and a half. Those naps were usually the result of not having slept during the night. I used to define naps as gently nodding off for a few minutes. But during my naps I dropped into the deepest sleep and woke with only the slightest sense of having rested.

I usually felt better after getting up, but I was never quite right. I felt like the remnants of a dream had been laid over the day like a veil, and I was caught halfway between darkness and light. I was often imbalanced or dizzy, and my motor skills suffered as my body struggled to keep up with my mind. I'd occasionally stagger into a doorframe or a piece of furniture. I would lose memory of the morning, as if I'd only dreamed about going to work.

I had to will myself into focus, because I was scheduled to work from 11:00 A.M. to 12:30 P.M. Then it was back home again for a four-hour nap. On those days I could remain awake in the afternoon, I tried to spend time with the children or do chores around the house. I was usually not very successful with either, for almost any exertion made me feel short of breath, generally lethargic, or brought on a crippling headache.

Friends Make the Difference

But as certain as I was of my physical limitations, I was just as sure of the unconditional support of my close friends and family. Through the difficult stages of the treatment they kept me sane. I recall the sage lesson in acceptance I received from two of my dearest friends, Melissa and Shubert Chang, whom I truly consider to be members of my family.

When I met Melissa in college, I was told she wore a prosthetic leg from her knee down. It's relevant that I had to be told—a missing limb isn't something you overlook, yet her artificial leg wasn't immediately noticeable in the way she carried herself. She had lost her leg in a motorcycle accident. She is married to a man named Shubert Chang, who also wears a prosthetic leg from the knee down, as the result of a motorcycle accident he suffered in high school. My family and the Changs share a bond as strong as any that exists between blood relatives, but even I forget that they have prosthetic legs. It is immediately apparent, however, that these strong Christian people have risen far above their circumstances, so far in fact as to make those circumstances negligible. They both work in the field of rehabilitation and prosthetics for children. Their positive attitudes give hope to all who are blessed enough to work with them or call them friends. Not once have I ever heard a complaint from Mel or Shubert about their legs. They have never in my presence asked, "Why me?" or expected special treatment. I believe that God is truly using these two solid Christians to do His work, and they certainly taught me a thing or two about faith.

I thought about the struggles they must have gone through—the physical pain, the rehabilitation, the emotional toll the accidents must have taken. If hepatitis C challenged my self-image, I could at least be thankful that I was physically whole. What strength and determination would it take to remain self-assured after the loss of a limb? Yet they had come through their respective experiences intact, their spirits restored, and in no uncertain terms they told me that I would make it too. Shubert and I spoke before my therapy began. He said, "Man you can beat this. With God, you can overcome anything. Anything. Just look at me." He laughed. I did look. I looked long and hard and I was thankful for his friendship.

Encouragement from Many

When I made my illness public, I was surprised by the enormous response I received from people I have never met. In a way, they knew me. I was in their living rooms and bedrooms every morning, helping them plan their day around the weather, telling them whether their children were going to school in severe conditions across the state. Thousands of people would be able to recognize me on the street, and any significant physical changes in me would immediately be noticed. I reasoned that if suddenly I lost my arms in a tragic accident and somehow managed to go back to work the next day, you can bet someone would want to know why I wasn't pointing to the weather wall with my usual enthusiasm.

I was told to expect side effects: nausea, hair loss, emotional distress, and changes in weight being chief among them. I believed that because viewers had always been so good to me, it was only fair to warn them. I'd also gotten sound advice from someone I believed was probably in the best position to understand my predicament.

When I discovered that I had hepatitis C, I scoured the Internet for every scrap of information I could find on treatment, side effects, and related statistics. Though helpful, most of what I found tended to be vaguely general and seemed to cover the same ground. I needed specifics.

A Call from Naomi Judd

One day, Roy Clem, the former general manager of ABC 33/40, my big boss and a dear friend, was standing in my office in the station's weather center. Aware of my condition and as one of the most understanding Christian gentlemen I have ever had the honor to know, he entertained my wild suggestion that I call Naomi Judd, the country music superstar who had overcome her battle against hepatitis C with inspirational success. Roy grinned and shot right back at me, "Why not?"

Sure, I thought. Why not call in the National Guard to find my car keys? You don't just call Naomi Judd! I told

Roy just what I thought of my own idea. "You'll never know if you don't try," he said. "What can she say? No? What will you lose if she does?"

He was right, of course, and I put a call in to her publicist, who agreed to pass along my request with all the cheeriness public relations people muster when dealing with the hopelessly oblivious. To my surprise I later discovered that Naomi knew me from the Nashville broadcast of the Rick and Bubba radio show. Her husband, Larry Strickland, called first.

Naomi was appearing on Star Search and writing a book, he told me, or she would have called instead. Larry was a musician to whom Naomi had been wed for more than 20 years, so he was a veteran of this treatment and had stood right next to Naomi as she traveled the highs and mostly lows it offers. He had taken on the same role that my wife Carol assumed, and his insight was crucial to understanding not only my own circumstances, but my family's as well. As the conversation carried on, I formed the impression that Larry was one of the kindest and most concerned people I had ever met. Although we had never spoken before and our first conversation was held over the phone, I felt this man cared for me and my situation. He was full of information and ideas on how to deal with hepatitis C. He was the first to encourage me to plan what I was going to do. He understood so many of the fears I was facing. We spent an hour on the phone, and during that time he gave me more strength and hope than I ever could have mustered alone. At the end he agreed to have Naomi call, and she did so right when I needed her most, the day after my first treatment.

When Naomi's call came I was sitting in a robe, shivering with chills, and feeling like an atom bomb had detonated between my ears. I truly believe Naomi was an angel sent to comfort me. We spoke at length about the disease and I was reminded that not only had she been a victim, she also was a trained nurse and knew as much about hepatitis C and the liver as anyone.

In addition to the pain and emotional turmoil the treatments caused me, I was downright embarrassed by being infected. I had done nothing to warrant shame, yet admitting that I had the illness was humiliating. Naomi understood this with absolute clarity, and during the course of our conversation she told me that she'd recently spoken to actor Pamela Anderson about how to handle the public reaction. She said, "Just tell people that you're sick and that it's nothing to be embarrassed about. Mark, just tell them that your close personal friend Naomi Judd said to let everyone know." We rang off and a sense of relief flowed through me just to know that I was better prepared to go public with my illness.

To this day, I have not forgotten what Naomi and Larry did for me: lifting me up while I was as down as I had ever been. Because of them and their support, I return the favor today to many others who contact me in search of answers and guidance. I'm a firm believer in the fact that if you pass it down the line and help someone in need, it will eventually come back to you. It's quite rewarding to me.

Going Public

Following Naomi's advice, I took notes from our conversation because, she warned me, I was not likely to remember much of it. Memory loss is another bonus in the disease's complimentary grab bag of side effects. Taking cues from those notes, I wrote this script for a story that aired on ABC 33/40 on October 28, 2002:

Hello. I'm Mark Prater. Many of you who watch me on Good Morning Alabama and the news at noon know I love to have fun. I love to make people laugh, but also take my job very seriously when it comes to severe weather in Alabama. But today I'm coming to you with a different kind of message.

I am battling an illness called hepatitis C, which is a blood-borne disease that kills your liver if left untreated. I've chosen to go public about my illness to explain any appearance changes I may go through over the next few months. Treatment or chemotherapy is very thorough and extensive to fight hepatitis C. Many of you may be familiar with Naomi Judd and Pamela Anderson. Well, Pamela is currently fighting the disease like me, and last week Naomi Judd called me in support, saying she is in remission. Unfortunately, though, before my diagnosis I had no clue what the disease was.

First, it's a blood-borne disease you can get through unscreened blood transfusions or contaminated needles. Many people in our country and around the world have been infected and don't know it, like me until a few months ago. I contracted the disease in 1985 through a blood platelet transfusion to save my life. Unfortunately, extensive blood screening was not a priority until the early 1990s.

I'm sharing this part of my very private life in hopes of helping others learn of this potentially deadly disease. I've asked God to be my physician during this battle with treatment, and with Him I will win.

I will continue to live my life as normally as possible. I thank you for your prayers and concern in advance. But I do ask that you allow my family and me the privacy we need to get through this fight.

If you've received blood transfusions before the early 1990s, gotten tattoos, or are a former IV drug user, check with your doctor to see if you should be tested. This disease knows no gender, race, or religious boundaries. In the next couple of years, this disease will be 5 times more widespread than AIDS and other blood-borne diseases, a sure health epidemic if a cure is not discovered.

I too am just learning about hepatitis C, so I may have difficulty answering questions you may have, but if you want to learn more, go to the Internet, log onto my friend Naomi Judd's web page NaomiJudd.com, or use any online search engine. You'll find a wealth of information out there.

Until I'm done with treatment and chemotherapy for this disease, my schedule will change from time to time. I hope you as my friends and family of viewers will allow me time to heal, to one day help others win the battle against hepatitis C.

Over the next several weeks, I came to discover just how many friends I had in the people I worked beside every day. John Oldshue and James Spann, my partners on the ABC 33/40 weather team, told me that no matter how much time I needed, they would be around to cover for me. Garry Kelly's continued support kept me from sinking into paranoia about my job prospects. He pulled me aside one day and assured me that I was doing great on the air and that my illness was barely noticeable. When pressed, he later admitted that it was in fact noticeable, but I was still doing well.

That support helped me push myself to be at work as often as possible and fight back against the disease with as much strength as I could muster. And strength often came from rest. I came home between shows to take a nap nearly every day to offset the insomnia caused by pain and the meds. I kept the pain at bay with prescription medication, Lortab 10, which I took one to four times a day depending on how I felt.

My co-anchor Keisa Sharpe was also a supportive prayer warrior for me. We'd pray before shows to keep God in the forefront. A parade of coworkers regularly came by my office to check on me or bring me water. Occasionally they would take note of my sorry condition and ask me if I needed to lie down. I found myself resting during commercial breaks, laying down on the set to fight dizziness or ever more frequent bouts of distraction. Everyone was patient with me. I insisted on coming to work, even on days when I could barely make it through the show without running to the bathroom to throw up.

Memory Loss

Particularly disappointing for me in the first few weeks of treatment was the steady erosion of my memory. I hadn't expected to forget the names of states. Geography is a meteorologist's best friend, and if you point to Missouri and say it's Idaho, then you have insulted the population of two states in addition to looking like an idiot.

Doing weather is unlike most other news. Anchors have scripts to follow and reporters file their stories already on tape. Meteorologists, on the other hand, rely on their instinctive knowledge of the weather and their memory to tell a story, holding the audience's attention without the safety net of a TelePrompTer. There were times when I would go blank, forgetting not only the names of places, but what the forecast held for Alabama. I usually found a way to dump out of the segment, chuckling about my obvious gaffe, but it became a sore point for me. How could I have pride in my work when my work just wasn't up to par?

Thankfully, Latrish Williford and Julie Echols, our morning show producers, were understanding and cool-headed at those times when I could not go on. In the middle of a show, if I was feeling disoriented, I'd get on the headset intercom and say, "I'm out, drop weather." It is no small request of a producer running a show with set commercial breaks and an out time that leads into network programming. My dropping out of the show leaves a significant hole in the broadcast into which the producers need to throw any scrap of news to fill it. It changes the scripts, the timing, and the camera work. And yet they adjusted without hesitation or complaint.

What I learned from these wonderful people is that in the midst of sorrow and despair, one of the most important things you can do for yourself is to remain open to help from those around you. In these circumstances it is tempting to narrow your circle of friends in the belief that either they will not understand your illness or they will pity you. People will surprise you with their compassion.

On the Radio

In my desire to go public with my hepatitis C, I felt I had a responsibility not only to the viewers who accepted me in their homes every day, but also to the listeners of the radio shows with which I am associated. To an attention junkie like me, being on television and radio represents the best of both worlds, and I am blessed with the opportunity to reach more people than I ever would reach in either medium alone. It was a dream I'd chased for years.

I got my start in television in the early 1990s by literally begging the news director of WTVY, the television power-house in Dothan, Alabama, for a weekend weather slot. After endless phone calls he told me that he did indeed have a position open and that I was the man to fill it. I took it, grateful for the job despite its cut-rate pay of five dollars an hour. It wasn't the money that mattered; it was the experience. By taking the position, I broke the oldest Catch-22 in the book: you can't get a job unless you have the experience, and you can't get the experience without a job. Now that I had my hooks in the business, I prepared myself to move on and move up.

In Dothan I also was a disc jockey at 99.7 WOOF-FM and pulled double duty working at WTVY-FM, the television station's radio arm. I was getting a taste of it all and learning how to improve my skills. My goal at the time was simple: I wanted to move to Montgomery and work for the station I'd watched as a young man. With patience and prayer I reached my goal, leapfrogged it in fact to become the weekend meteorologist at Birmingham's ABC affiliate, WBRC.

While there I noted that the station's chief meteorologist, James Spann, was doing radio forecasts daily. I wanted to duplicate his success in tackling both media. In fact, he was so successful at it that no one else in town thought that any other weatherman could compete against him. Consequently no one took the bait.

But in 1996 a new station in Birmingham was accepting applications for weather staff. James went to the new station, ABC 33/40, and put in a good word for me with his bosses. I got the job as a morning meteorologist, but that didn't stop me from pushing for a radio slot. I thought of all the extra exposure a radio job would represent and I inquired after potential opportunities in town. There were none to be found, or so I thought.

I'd started speaking at local schools, and I was spinning the radio dial on a trip to Anniston, Alabama. That was when I heard the voice of Bill "Bubba" Bussey and Rick Burgess, hosts of the Rick and Bubba Show. At the time, they were on a small FM station in Gadsden, but they were undeniably funny and a breath of fresh air in the over-hyped, frequently crass morning drive time format.

Their humor and spark stuck with me throughout the trip home and I convinced myself that the Rick and Bubba Show was a place I could call home on the radio. I wanted desperately to be a part of the team in some small way. I called and pitched the idea to them on a whim, and to my surprise they accepted. Sure, they said, come aboard. I did their weather breaks and they let me hang around for chat from 7:45 to 8 A.M.

At the beginning of our relationship we swapped similar stories about how no one had wanted me on the radio, just as no one in Birmingham was willing to produce and air a televised version of their radio show. But we grew and became more attractive as a product. With every boost in their ratings and with every new contract agreement, Rick and Bill stood fast against moving without me. It was a marriage of professionals that is still strong after eight years. I've since been awarded the Associated Press's Best Weathercaster in the state. I nabbed an Emmy and an Edward R. Murrow Award for live weather coverage. This is a relationship I truly feel God put into my life to help me in this industry.

By 1999, Bill and Rick had moved to Birmingham, and I was doing weather radio for their sister stations in town. I went in search of new radio opportunities. I fell in step with WDJC, a powerhouse Christian radio station in the city, which hosted a morning show featuring Dave Mack and Mark Congleton. With every broadcast, these boys shattered the stereotype of Bible-thumping, fire-and-brimstone-breathing, snake-charming Christians by mixing God's Word with sly humor. I went on board with the same attitude. I did their forecasts and spent a few minutes chatting on the air, much in the way I did on Rick and Bubba's show. Mark and Mack's format was a huge success in Birmingham and I was able to remain in the company of Christian broadcasters.

On the Radio

I'd made the decision to announce my illness to the television audience, but of course the word spread quickly, and before I had properly planned it I knew that I would have to make similar statements to the radio audiences as well.

I prepped my coworkers on both shows about what I wanted to say. They were supportive and we knew that a public announcement also meant a public recovery as long as I stayed on the air. They assured me that God would prevail.

The radio offered a unique way of handling the side effects. Behind the microphone you can paint an entirely new self-portrait. You may have a face for radio, but your voice and your personality can lift you beyond any physical drawbacks. You can be charming and persuasive, you can throw barbs at your critics and roses at your fans, and they will love you for it. And if only you could win the approval of your bosses, you could do it all in the comfort of your pajamas.

I asked that Rick and Bubba, and Mark and Mack, go on with the radio shows as if I was perfectly healthy. I did not want to make either show a forum for my disease. I wasn't looking for a soapbox and I certainly didn't want to stand up under public scrutiny any more than I had to. I asked the public to respect my privacy and told them that I would keep them updated on my progress. In this way I was able to focus my mind on the job at hand. It helped that I could call in to the radio shows from my office at the television station. In this way my daily routine was only minimally adjusted.

Radio offered me the opportunity to escape, even for the briefest periods of time. I didn't have to worry about looking pale or tired or weak. If my voice could hold, then I could continue as normal, make a few jokes, and momentarily forget that I was undergoing therapy. But there were reminders, of course.

I recall that I was chatting with Mark and Mack on their show when I felt a wave of nausea sweep over me. I fought against it and willed it away with enormous effort. But I had scheduled both shows so that Rick and Bubba immediately followed Mark and Mack. I barely had room to breathe between the two, and in the rush to get on the air with Rick and Bubba, the nausea returned. I held on for the first few minutes, but in the middle of my time slot it hit me like a slug from a rifle.

I remember abruptly saying, "I've got to go guys. Lots of love and we'll see you soon." I barely made it off the phone. I ran to the bathroom and stayed there until the heaving passed. This scenario would repeat itself again and again throughout my therapy, but I was grateful for the blessings and the encouragement given to me by people in the audiences.

Privacy

I wanted no part of what I imagined would be a self-serving campaign during which I proclaimed my disease to all who might listen. I did not want to become the voice for hepatitis C for the people who saw me on TV and heard me on the radio. I watched this scenario unfold for Michael J. Fox when he announced that he had Parkinson's disease. He took the initiative as a national celebrity and went on speaking tours and published a book about his daily battle against the degenerative illness. Suddenly people took notice of Parkinson's because it had attacked someone we all knew and loved. Perhaps because I felt embarrassed about my hepatitis C, my first reaction was to accept condolences and progress through treatment in relative privacy. I was glad to see Mr. Fox elicit such an enthusiastic response, but I could never achieve for hep C what he did for Parkinson's, and in fact, I didn't want to.

I wondered about others with hepatitis C. Was the disease suddenly more relevant because I had it? What about the millions of others who are suffering who aren't on television or who aren't heard on the radio every day? Aren't they just as important? In fact, on the whole I think I was relatively lucky—I had contracted the type two genotype, which responds better to therapy and has a shorter treatment span. There are countless people who know more about suffering and pain and depression in association with the disease than I do. So what makes me special? I wanted to be able to get through it, get through it with character, get through it with faith, keep my head up, and be an example people might see and say, "This is doable. He did it this way, he fought through it." And I thought I would one day sit down and tell the story of what really went on behind the scenes. But I didn't want to become a spokesman for the disease.

In the end I became an advocate without realizing it, and that was probably the best way for it to happen. When people in my audiences found out, they began to write me, either to offer encouragement or to ask for it. I answered as many e-mails and letters as I could, I encouraged new patients, I accepted their prayers, and I set out to prove that the disease was not some hulking, immovable obstacle. I wanted to show that I could fight against it and not let it consume my life.

Support

When I finally broke the news of my illness, ABC 33/40 and the radio stations were awash with uplifting messages of hope and sympathy, and of prayers and support. I could not have been more pleased by the public reaction. Bushels of mail came pouring in to the station after my report. I think God must have hired a few extra angels to handle the enormous outpouring of prayer I was receiving. Churches put me on their daily prayer lists, and letter after letter came with encouraging passages from the Bible. Over the course of my treatments I compiled hundreds of e-mails, many of which I found particularly useful.

I discovered a running theme through the messages I read, and to which I responded. People who had contracted the virus and those who loved them enough to care for them were equally afraid. They didn't know what to expect. They wanted someone to tell them in plain English how bad it was going to be.

I also discovered that the patients themselves were not always the ones who reached out to me. The initial contact usually came from a relative, and I knew why. Hepatitis C is not a "sympathetic" disease. In many cases patients who may have contracted the disease through no fault of their own feel shamed by the admission that they have it. They equate it with drug use and shady tattoo parlors and unprotected sex with multiple partners. This shame only helps the virus. A patient who remains silent and uneducated about the disease has a greater chance of transmitting it to someone else, who may feel equally embarrassed and through their silence spread the disease even further.

You wonder how people are going to judge you. In those supportive e-mails and letters, people admitted that they did IV drugs in college but they were now upstanding members of their communities, churchgoers, productive members of the workforce. Doctors and nurses called and wrote, telling about how they had contracted it occupationally. I had a surgeon who wrote me and asked that we stay in touch. We were starting treatment at the same time and he wanted to know what I was going through.

Hepatitis C is an equal opportunity virus; it holds no biases. No amount of money or privilege will make you immune. It plucks victims from every rung of the social ladder. I tell people that hepatitis C is vile but that doesn't mean those who have acquired it are. Any disease that conspires to take your life is vile. I tell them that they're not alone. There are a lot of us that have it. Over the next several years many more people will have discovered they have it. No matter who they are, they will be shocked and saddened, perhaps frightened that acquiring hepatitis C is a death sentence.

I want to tell people, "Here's the good news: this is beatable and we can treat this. Here's even better news: you're going to be able to survive."

Prayers

One e-mail came from a gentleman I never met and have not heard from since, but we continued to exchange e-mails over a period of time during which I realized what an isolating effect a debilitating disease can have on a person. This man was a fellow hepatitis C patient, though he'd gone through the treatment already and was therefore greatly informed. He knew my ailments as well as I did. Headaches? He'd had them. Joint pain? Yes, as if someone had put his knees and knuckles in a vise. Nausea? Are you kidding? Memory loss? It came with the territory, and there were some experiences during the six months of treatment that I would never recall. He described the metallic taste of the ribavirin pills, and his shortness of breath after minimal exertion. On the one hand his accuracy was frightening. But it was comforting as well. By reaching out to me, he let me know what to expect and personified in a real way the vast number of people affected by hepatitis C.

He admitted to me early in our correspondence that he'd had no one in which to confide during his treatment. What a lonely journey his must have been. It is disconcerting enough to suffer through months of illness. It is even more so without a network of friends and family to carry you through the darkest times. In my position as an on-air personality, my safety net was expanding from my family to the friends who supported me from afar.

Strangers offered me the most inspiring words of courage, many of them from Scripture. I have saved a number of these and recall one that was especially heartfelt. It came to me before one of my scheduled treatments, and read:

Prayer Request—Chemo today, 10 A.M.
• *Pray that God's Word is proclaimed to*

glorify Him and that His promise of healing is completely manifest in my body and life.

• *Pray that the symptoms in my body do not negate the fact that Jesus came to bring us life and life abundantly (John 10:10).*

• *Pray that I will meditate on His Word and confess my sins and that the Holy Spirit will give me wisdom and revelation in the knowledge of Jesus Christ and His spiritual, mental, emotional, and physical healing power.*

• *Pray that I will put Proverbs 4:20–22 foremost in my life. "My son, attend to my words; incline thine ear unto my sayings. Let them not depart from thine eyes; keep them in the midst of thine heart. For they are life unto those that find them, and health to all their flesh."*

• *As I take chemo, pray that this toxic drug will kill all the afflicted cells in my body but that God will protect all the good cells— that they may remain healthy, thereby proclaiming God's promise found in the following Scriptures:*

    Mark 16:18— "They shall take up serpents; and if they drink any deadly thing, it shall not hurt them; they shall lay hands on the sick, and they shall recover."

Luke 10:19— "Behold, I give unto you power to tread on serpents and scorpions, and over all the power of the enemy; and nothing shall by any means hurt you."

• *Pray that my testimony will be:*

Mark 11:24— "Therefore I say unto you, What things soever ye desire, when ye pray, believe that ye receive them, and ye shall have them."

Psalm 30:2— "O LORD my God, I cried unto thee, and thou hast healed me."

Psalm 103:2–3— "Bless the LORD, O my soul, and forget not all his benefits: who forgiveth all thine iniquities; who healeth all thy diseases."

These words remain as uplifting today as they were when I first read them. My faith was strengthened when I discovered how powerful prayer can be. The simple passages eased my pain and shone a light of hope into the darkness that too often threatened to engulf me.

Both Carol and I prayed to God for help. Carol prayed day after day, "Please take this from him, Lord. Please don't make him go through all of this." Scriptures like these assured me that many before me had traveled the path I traveled.

Every one of these beautiful Scriptures was written thousands of years ago. Yet they all alluded to the same thing: *Child, I will not fail you! For he who keeps Me first will be rewarded and succeed in any struggle he may be facing*. God is always, always there. He may let us learn along the way, and in so doing we stumble and fall and rise only to stumble again, but through prayer we bolster our faith. He will surround us with angels and shower us with blessings, especially in our time of greatest need. He will place people in our path who will offer us exactly what we need at exactly the time we need it. Through prayer we believe ever more that God is omnipresent. He will never, ever leave our side.

I found that as my therapy continued, I would have to rely on faith even more, and that it would be tested.

Chapter Six
Hitting Bottom

I had been warned that my mood would darken as a result of the treatments, and I had seen that darkening in action. My family and friends were exceptionally understanding, but even now I feel I must ask for their forgiveness, as in the Lord's Prayer—*Forgive us our trespasses as we forgive those who trespass against us.*

Yet the farther into the treatment I went, the more of a challenge the therapy and its effect on my mood became as I tried to maintain my faith in God's redemptive power.

Before I started therapy, Larry Strickland and Naomi Judd gave me fantastic advice, not only in the matter of exposing news of my disease to the public, but also in telling me what to expect, and what might be done to combat the most difficult aspects of treatment. Larry recommended that I see a psychiatrist. Initially, this did not sound like sensible advice. Hepatitis C is a virus, fought with antiviral drugs. I didn't think I would need a head doctor. But perusing the information I came across while researching the disease, I found repeated references to depression. One very clear and rather disturbing explanation read, "Severe psychiatric adverse events, including depression, psychoses, aggressive behavior, hallucinations, violent behavior (suicidal ideation, suicidal attempts, suicides), and rare instances of homicidal ideation have occurred during combination Rebetol/Intron therapy, both in patients with and without a previous psychiatric disorder." [Willis C. Maddrey, M.D. and Eugene R. Schiff, M.D. *The Hepatitis Workbook: A Guide to Living with Chronic Hepatitis B and C*, 2001]. It was clear that the disease was attacking my mind as well as my body and that my mind would require treatment as well.

Dr. Stacy Siegel, the psychiatrist Carol and I ended up visiting, has an office near our home in Homewood, Alabama. Her sunny disposition and beaming smile were immediately engaging. It was important to me that she was experienced in treating disease-related depression, and I found her comfortably knowledgeable on the subject of interferon and its effects on the psyche. During our consultation we discussed our marriage and life with four children. Routine questions with routine answers, or so I thought. I felt that it was important to impress her and Carol, and I believe I put on a little bit of a show that was clearly transparent to both of them. Carol was the first to see some changes in my personality. As it turns out, I was the one blithely unaware of those changes.

I paid little attention to the way I had dressed for the consultation. Carol walked in as I was putting the finishing touches on my outfit: black jeans, black button down shirt, black shoes, black socks, and a black leather jacket. "Hey, Johnny Cash," she said, "are you ready to go?"

I smirked and said, "Yeah. But, that's not that funny. I like this setup. It makes me look thin, doesn't it?"

She smiled and said, "Sure does, honey—you look great!"

I was used to wearing well cut suits with brightly colored power ties to make a fashionable statement every day on the air. I later realized that my drastic change in wardrobe might have been a sign that all was not well. All too often, especially with a debilitating illness, patients can't see the depression coming on; the changes may be subtle to the patients, but the signs may present themselves quite plainly to those around them. My family had noticed sharp changes in my personality even before I discovered I had the disease. I became subject to violent mood swings. I lost my temper faster than usual, I was rude to Carol and the children in a way that was often unforgivable, and now I was dressing like the Prince of Darkness. I might as well have carried around a billboard declaring my altered condition during that first visit.

After the consultation the doctor prescribed the antidepressant Lexapro. I was not happy about it and I fought to keep my temper in check. I had tried to put a positive spin on my condition. Things were not so bad, I tried to convince the doctor. Sure, the therapy was crippling and I wanted to die and I was constantly taking my frustrations out on friends and family, but I was coping with it as well as could be expected, wasn't I? Did I need to be shown again that I was a weakling who had to depend on drugs for a sense of well-being? You see how twisted my thoughts were at the time.

Antidepressants are not instant cures. It takes a matter of weeks before the drugs can successfully infiltrate your system and affect your mood. Despite my concerns I was pleased with the initial results. My mood improved. I directed fewer tirades at my wife and kids. I had more patience at work. I was set to get the lifestyle I loved back on track. But soon I discovered that something was wrong with our chosen medication. In my case, instead of gently correcting my mood, it eventually altered it to such a degree as to render me nearly emotionless. If the disease had caused my heart rate to race, for example, the antidepressant silenced it, as cold and still as death.

After a time I had become accustomed to my own mood swings; I knew what to expect even if I couldn't rationalize it later. But this new feeling, this flat emotionless response to everything, was something new. As the treatment progressed, I began to realize that the things that normally affected me deeply became less and less meaningful. I was turning to stone.

When I was a reporter in Montgomery, I covered a story in Enterprise, Alabama, that stuck with me for days. The cameraman, a good friend of mine named Jeff Harrison, and I were on the scene of a hostage situation that went horribly wrong. In the interest of time, Jeff thought it best to send video back to the news station while the scene was still unfolding. He left me with the camera, which was pointed at the hostage, an innocent 18-year-old girl, and the suspect, who were approximately 120 feet away. I continued to film the scene, zooming in close just when a police sniper's bullet ripped through the girl and the suspect, killing them both. I had a front row seat to their executions.

It took me several days to put my emotions in order, and to this day the image of them taking that fatal hit is indelibly burned into my memory. How would I have reacted if I had been on the medication when the shooting occurred? The answer frightened me.

Working in the news business, one finds no shortage of opportunities to reflect on unfortunate incidents. I would hear a story of a child drowning in the pool during our newscast. Didn't affect me. Particularly since I've become a father, I find myself thinking about how I would feel if one of my children were tragically taken from me. I'd wonder, *Lord, what if that had been Cole or Trinity?* Under normal circumstances, I can't bear to even consider it. But on this medication, nothing mattered to me. I could watch those stories without a flicker of concern. There was a problem there, a problem that had begun to affect my marriage.

Therapy can test even the strongest of families. Under normal circumstances we each may face the daily conflicts of raising children, keeping a home, and paying bills. But these seemingly ordinary challenges are amplified by the stress and strain of chemotherapy when a patient's nerves are stretched to the limit. As a result, many couples have fallen victim to the adversity that a person undergoing treatment can create. I was no better. Furthermore, I felt that my actions were without consequence. It didn't matter to me what I said in anger or who I hurt in the process.

Tantrums

Carol reminded me of a typical example of one of my outbursts, which usually concluded with her in tears on the phone with my mother, threatening to put me out of the house. My rants would end far afield from where I began. I would stalk through the kitchen in a foul mood and I might feel crumbs of cereal under my bare feet. In a house with four children you're lucky not to have the entire contents of the refrigerator laid out on the floor in a rotting heap. Carol could sweep the kitchen four times a day and there might still be a mess to clean. That would be the rational way to accept a few crumbs here and there. But I wasn't being rational. I would find Carol and bark at her: "This house is never cleaned up! It's nasty and horrible. I'm so embarrassed, I gave you this wonderful house, this wonderful neighborhood, you're here all day long, you don't have anything to do, and you are so unappreciative."

In my mind the connection was made from crumbs on the floor, to a dirty house, to an unappreciative wife; from an angry comment about the housework to a personal attack on Carol. I would issue an ultimatum. "If you don't like it, just leave. Leave the kids here with me and you just leave."

In Carol's defense, I can only imagine the incredible restraint she had to keep from packing my bags and sending me on my way. Of course, I didn't see it that way when she would quietly nod her head and say, "Okay, Mark. You're right. I'll clean it up." I'd think of it as a victory. I just wanted the crumbs up off the floor, because I was sick of walking through there barefooted and stepping on garbage.

In fact, the only victory I could have claimed was that I had married someone who recognized that I was a different person than the one she'd pledged to love. Carol had decided at some point that she would simply let me rage. She would yield, no matter how belligerent I behaved, and she refused to argue. She began to recognize when a particularly nasty temper was brewing, in the same way that I can look up into the sky and see a storm ahead. What would be the point in arguing with a thundercloud? It would not hear you, it certainly wouldn't respond to your pleas, no matter how logical your argument might seem, and the longer you stood in the rain, the more miserable you would become. Like a storm, she let it pass, as difficult as that probably was. Carol does not take things lying down. But she also knew that, invariably, when the storm passed and I regained my composure, that I would feel an enormous amount of guilt.

In the middle of my treatment, when I was making everyone miserable, Carol printed out the lyrics to Naomi's song, *Love Can Build a Bridge,* telling me in her own way that she would not be put off by the little demon I let loose in our marriage. I read the words and found them so comforting that I posted them at my bedside and read them again and again when I was at my lowest.

> *I'd gladly walk across the desert*
> *With no shoes upon my feet*
> *To share with you the last bite*
> *Of bread I had to eat*
> *I would swim out to save you*
> *In your sea of broken dreams*
> *When all your hopes are sinkin'*
> *Let me show you what love means*

It was a blessing to feel the depth of Carol's commitment. Yet therapy had created a new Mark Prater, whose temper was out of control. I apologized as often as I could and I thank God for Carol's understanding. She knew I didn't mean the things I said, but you have to really love someone with all of your heart to stand in front of the barrage of verbal abuse I threw at her. Here she was, caring for me at every turn, warming me under a mountain of quilts while cooling my fevers with ice, carrying me to bed, administering every medicine, cooking every meal, staying up with me late at night, accompanying me through my insomnia, and getting the kids ready for school early in the morning, never asking for any comfort, never expecting any praise, and I gave her anger in return.

I remember sitting at the computer or watching television after a tantrum, thinking, "I can't believe I just said that to my wife, my best friend. I can't believe I did it, but I really don't care." I was two people in one body, shocked and amazed that I could dole out such venom, and simultaneously detached from any real concern about Carol's feelings.

Fortunately, Dr. Siegel understood what I was dealing with. She was aware of several cases in which patients had exhibited similar side effects. I wish I had known before I agreed to take the medication. Armed now with knowledge, I decided to switch to a new antidepressant, Wellbutrin, and within a few weeks I felt balance once again returning to my life. I felt things more deeply, though not so deeply that they affected my rationality. It was important to maintain an even keel, and the Wellbutrin helped immensely. I scheduled a monthly office visit to ensure that I stayed on track, since no medicine is an absolute cure-all, and, as I expected, the depression came creeping back time and again to wrest control of my emotions. It was the randomness that made it so difficult. One moment you believed you had everything under control and then in a flash you were that person with the short fuse, the rude, careless person you dreaded meeting again. The doctor reminded me that we could keep it under control with a steady schedule of medicine and psychiatric checkups. It was good plan, except that the equation was missing an important element. In the discussions regarding my mental health we had failed to mention God. I didn't expect the good doctor to minister to me in the way my pastor would, because that simply wasn't her job. It was my responsibility to keep God in my life throughout the entire ordeal, and as I progressed through therapy the strongest opponent I found in the battle for my Christian strength was the person I saw in the mirror every day. This is what depression does to you.

Friends and family unfamiliar with the condition may be tempted to cheer you up. They may bring flowers or send cards, and invariably they will be disappointed with the results. Some may take the hard-line approach and tell you to "just get over it." "Come on," they'll say. "What's your problem?" The answer won't be easy. How do you explain that you just want to be left alone all of the time, or that you don't feel joy over the things that used to make you smile? You may have difficulty expressing your feelings because these emotions don't come with a handbook of simple explanations. I often felt that I was just not happy. I had a cloud hanging over me and even the most inoffensive remarks made me feel bad. I felt like I couldn't make anything go right. Too often I offended someone over something seemingly insignificant. Every small problem is a big problem, and the big problems are insurmountable, the kind that make you flinch as if physically struck by a hammer blow. With each blow your perspective on God's role in the journey toward recovery is thrown farther and farther out of kilter.

Anger at God

As time went on, I began abandoning my daily prayer, another sign that I was under the influence of the disease. I am normally adamant about everyday prayer. It is as natural and as routine as bathing, a cleansing process to prepare your body and soul for the rigors of daily life. I feel it's vital to thank God for every blessing and ask for His guidance on how to serve Him each and every day. I give Him everything I have, offering Him my life, my soul, my family, and all of our worldly possessions. But in the shadows of depression I tended to put my gratitude aside in favor of resentment. It is said that the ones you love are the ones you hurt the most, and if you love God, then He becomes a primary target for your rage and your disappointment, your fears and your doubts.

I recall telling Carol on too many occasions how God was really not there for me. I was tired of Him using me for His purpose and witness. Why should I have to go through so much abuse every day and look the way I do? Where was God when I became so weak that I began taking note of the number of stairs in my house? Going up those stairs was a hurdle. I counted them with each step and knew in short order that between the television room and the kitchen there stood sixteen stairs. There were another sixteen between my bedroom and the children's rooms upstairs. For months I couldn't tuck them in bed. I would literally sit halfway up the stairs until I could get my breath back. That made me furious. Once, while still undergoing therapy, I felt particularly industrious. I went to clean out the garage. It turned out to be a bad idea. I couldn't complete the job and I became winded after only a short amount of time. Back in the house I tried to climb the stairs to the kitchen and I made it to the second step, which is where Carol found me with my arms wrapped around my head, trying to catch my breath. "I just can't make it any further," I told her. I just sat there, as Carol recalls, with my head on the stairs and my fanny in the air. "Don't touch me. Be here, but don't touch me," I said.

Thinking of how absurd I must have looked at that moment, I turned around and looked at Carol and said, "One of these days I'm going to look back at this and think it's really funny. But it's not funny right now."

I had always taken pride in my health and fitness. I was athletic and as often as I could I pushed myself to the limit in competitive sports. Now I was weak, out of shape. I never actually turned my back on God. I allowed that His will is unquestionable, but I didn't have to like it. I was angry and confused. I felt like I had slipped from the top of the world and that it had been a long way down. God could have stopped that descent into darkness with a simple blessing, in the way that we might wave our hands or snap our fingers. I believed I had prayed enough for deliverance, and that I had suffered enough. I put God on the back burner. I began to lose interest in my personal quiet time with Him. I played the role in front of my children, outwardly displaying the characteristics of faith and reverence, but as an actor on the stage I could turn it on or off at will and my heart wasn't in it. I wanted my children to believe that God remained my spiritual light to guide us through to the end, even if I started to believe that the light had gone out. I felt like a hypocrite.

I spent the greater part of the treatment regimen wondering about God's role in my life, sometimes fully aware of His presence, and at other times certain that I had been left behind. At my lowest point I was sure I was alone, and frankly I didn't care. I imagined God on His throne in heaven, watching me, judging me based on my actions, which I felt were no fault of my own. He'd cursed me with this terrible condition and had left me defenseless, like a turtle on its back. Looking back, I can see now that He was allowing me to stumble and fall, but He was there all along.

I remember reading a poem my mother had stitched for me called *Footprints in the Sand*. The author, Mary Stevenson, wrote it in 1936 when she was only 14 years old. It has since been widely published on posters, coffee mugs, calendars, and in greeting cards and religious materials. It was a parable of one man's journey through life with Jesus. In the poem Stevenson writes about a man who walked along the shore of beach with Jesus and saw his life flash before him. He noted that during the low points of his life that he could detect only one set of footprints in the sand, and wondered why Jesus had left him in his time of need. Jesus answered that when the man had been at his lowest, He had carried him. This poem was extremely inspirational for me at a time when I felt it was useless counting on God. Through it all, while I remained discouraged and broken, God was working through me, my family, and my friends in ways I had never even considered. Most importantly, He blessed me with a wife who was patient and understanding beyond comprehension. I truly believe that without her strength, our marriage would be a memory today.

God also placed in my path one of finest persons in the world, Scott Patten. Scott's wife, battling multiple sclerosis, was treated with interferon for five years. Today Connie is one of the kindest, most pleasant people I have ever had the pleasure to meet. But I got my first impression of her while she was undergoing treatment, and only now can I see in myself what I saw in her. She took Scott to task for every perceived misstep and seemed to have no regard for anyone's feelings other than her own. It was difficult to watch the two of them and at the time I could not image having to endure the constant conflict that must have been present in their home. I know now that I became a monster under the influence of interferon for six months, a mere fraction of the time Scott and Connie faced treatment for MS. I truly wondered how he stayed with her. The answer was simple, of course. He stayed with her because he loved her. He had faith—faith in her and faith in God.

Connie is no longer taking interferon. She is such an incredibly kind and fun person to be around, it's almost as if the interferon had possessed her body and mind during those difficult years. Her anger is gone. Her insecurity and fears are gone, and she and Scott have a life again.

Scott has been an inspiration for me and for Carol. He has defined true love. He fought through all of the hardship with patience and an even-tempered perspective. Carol has been no less of a warrior. Through it all she loved me dearly and I can't begin to tell her how much it meant to me that she stood by my side, honoring our wedding vows, caring for me for better or worse, through sickness and health. She held up her end of the deal, and since we fought this battle against hepatitis C, I've vowed even more strongly to God that I will hold up my end. Without God in our marriage, lives, and home, we never would have survived the biggest crisis we've faced yet in our marriage. All along, God was there, carrying me, carrying us both; three sets of footprints in the sand and His alone during our greatest trials.

Thankfully, the antidepressant curbed my darkest thoughts. Some patients have been known to contemplate suicide. But in some very real ways I became someone I am not comfortable recalling. Here the role of family becomes not only one of support, but as a mender of fences; family becomes a mirror into which patients should be forced to look and examine themselves. Carol was that mirror for me.

Relating to My Children

In the first three months of treatment, the most unpleasant aspects of my personality became more pronounced. I am a strict father. Since Cole became old enough to speak, he has addressed me with a respectful "sir," as I did to my father. Madison and Trinity, my young daughters, also know the extent of my discipline. I've always believed that children require a standard against which to measure right and wrong, and that the journey through life is made that much more arduous without proper strength of will. Yet under treatment I became an unbearable disciplinarian. I assigned blame at will, found faults where there were none, and against my Christian beliefs I lost control of my temper and my language. I swore like a sailor, and even while doing so the part of my mind that still functioned rationally wondered, "Why can't I control myself? Why am I hurting my family? They're the only ones standing between me and insanity." But knowing I was doing wrong somehow failed to rectify it, and I was soon back to lashing out at will.

The girls tried to deal with the effects of my hepatitis C in their own way. Their tendency was to mother me, sit with me as often and for as long as possible. They seemed to know instinctively, the way children do, that Daddy was somewhere inside the raging monster I had become, and they tried with every ounce of sweetness they had to draw me out. Carol was the first to notice that the relationship I had with my children was failing. "You're not letting them care for you," Carol told me. "You're not letting them sit with you. You don't do things with them like they want. This is Madison's and Trinity's way of showing you they love you and are worried." I knew she was right, and when the realization came, I was remorseful of the quality time I had lost with my children, but I vowed to be more patient, and more understanding.

I might have followed my children's example. They showed enormous strength when I was at my worst, and my weakest.

We learned early that, over the course of this treatment, there would be a series of setbacks when we least expect it. We went home for the Thanksgiving holiday. Family gatherings can be as exasperating as they are energizing, but I was thankful for the opportunity to spend time with them. As I took the wheel on the hour-long drive down to Prattville, I felt, at least for the moment, that I was simply another traveler on one of the busiest holidays of the year, visiting their folks and celebrating their blessings together. We had a wonderful evening catching up on the latest news, and I answered their questions about my health. I began to fade during the ride back. In the final 20 minutes of the drive home, I stopped and asked Carol to take over. I hopped in the passenger seat of the Yukon and dropped into a sleep so deep as to appear unconscious, according to Carol.

I was scheduled for a treatment on the following day. We chose to go out for dinner instead of cooking and we left the treatment until after our evening out; if I planned it earlier in the day I would have had to cancel dinner, and I wanted to maintain a regular life with my family. Additionally, Carol and I planned to regularly administer the interferon shots when the house was quiet, after the children were in bed. But all through dinner I remained preoccupied with the treatment. I dreaded it, as I did every Friday.

As usual, I managed to keep myself busy until the very last possible moment. Carol mixed the solution and gave me the shot like a professional. I could not have asked for better care. And as part of our ritual we stayed up afterwards, just the two of us. It was our way to hold off the inevitable sickness that followed Friday night shots. I never wanted to go to bed because I knew how I would feel the next morning even if I managed to get a good night's sleep. Carol stayed up with me on most nights, refusing to go to bed until I did.

That Friday night, sitting beside my wife an hour after the treatment, I felt the medication go to work. I was suddenly overwhelmed by dizziness and nausea, but there was something distinctly different about this attack, as if the virus and the interferon had conspired against me, reaching into a new bag of tricks to torture me. I saw flashes before my eyes, and hallucinations. One very clear trick of the eye convinced me that someone had just crossed the room, a dark figure comprised of shadow that had moved past me up the stairs to the kitchen. I followed, trying to hold down the contents of my stomach. I staggered up the last set of stairs and lunged at the kitchen sink where everything I had eaten was forced out. The strain of it burst some blood vessels in my eyes and at the end of it I looked and felt as if I had gone three rounds in a heavyweight fight and had lost.

I felt all physical control slip away. It was as if a puppeteer had suddenly let the strings go lax and I collapsed one body part at a time until I could no longer support my own weight. I hit the floor hard, landing on my tail bone. My head slammed against the cabinet under the sink. Carol rushed from the television room to find me sliding into a prone position on the floor. I was conscious but unable to bring my arms and legs in line. They weren't taking orders and I felt in no condition to give them.

In a panic, Carol ran upstairs to wake Cole, who at 11 years old was already tall enough to look me in the eye. They found me on the floor and carried me to my bed. I was murmuring, Carol later told me, though what I mumbled will forever remain a mystery. I awoke the next morning in pain from what I gathered was a combination of the fall, the Rebetol and the Peg-Intron. But more hurtful was the embarrassment I felt having been so helpless the night before. Carol was there when I opened my eyes. "Where's Cole?" I asked. She called him into the room and I sheepishly sat up.

"Son," I said, "I'm a little embarrassed. I guess I looked pretty weak last night. I'm sorry you had to pick your Daddy up off of the floor. I'm stronger than that, you know."

What Cole said to me next will stay with me always. He turned toward me, pinning me with those beautiful teddy bear eyes. "Daddy, you're not weak. Don't worry about it."

I smiled at him. "Thanks son, I love you!"

"I love you too, Dad. Just so you know, I'll go anywhere, at anytime, to help pick you up. I'll always be there for you!"

It took every ounce of self-control to keep from breaking down in front of him. I covered it with a joke, of course. "You're a good boy...I mean, young man." I was able to stem the tide of tears until just after he left the room, but no longer than that, and I privately thanked God for the blessing of my son.

I believe my children and my wife were sent to me by God not only as people with which to share my love, but as teachers. During this difficult period I learned so much more from them than I could have ever expected. But of all the things I learned, one of the most valuable lessons was that family members have to be as prepared as the patient for the physically and emotionally draining recovery. Granted, the side effects of treatment for hepatitis C vary from patient to patient, but emotional distress is common to nearly each and every one. People tend to lash out when they are in pain and the people at whom they lash out are usually those closest to them. Fortunately, my best friend, my wife Carol, knew what to expect because we were given very sound advice, and therefore we were able to prepare my family for the worst. Carol knew that I would say things I didn't mean, though I'm not at all sure that knowing in advance made it any easier for her. If her patience wore thin at times, I was rarely aware of it. I discovered that she often came behind me, cleaning up the mess my errant angry comments left behind, making it right as often as she could.

She wrote notes for me, knowing that, thanks to the therapy, I would forget the simplest things: names, numbers, addresses, even our own phone number.

While you are actively participating in your own torture in the interest of getting well, you get tired of hurting. You get tired of losing hair, tired of not sleeping. Your body is not happy that you continue to treat it so poorly. Trust me, my body spoke loudly and clearly for six months. I remember Dr. Fallon telling me, "Hey, we're still learning about interferon and ribavirin. We're making progress, but try to remember, we're still discovering what this will do to your mind and body." He addressed me with a straightforward approach, his hallmark. "Look, Mark, try to understand, *I'm* doing this to you—not Carol, not you, not your kids. It's me! This is going to create lots of problems and things may get better, but you can certainly count on them getting worse. Just hang in there. You're going to beat this, man! Okay?"

Good News

For a moment I believed him. It helped that my blood work was consistently positive and that at 12 weeks Dr. Fallon called me in for tests. The markers for liver disease are raised enzymes aspartate aminotransferase (AST) and alanine aminotransferase (ALT) in your bloodstream. Also, hepatitis C is referred to as an RNA virus, because it has ribonucleic acid as its genetic material. To gauge how a patient is responding to therapy, doctors typically check for hepatitis C RNA, which when the virus is no longer present shows up at a barely detectable level. An RNA test so early in the treatment is not part of the normal regimen, but the weeks leading up to it had been so miserable for me Carol that Dr. Fallon wanted to see if the therapy was working.

I tried to go back to work in the week before the test. I was sick, my voice was crummy, and I felt horrible, coughing and having chills and fever. Finally, Garry Kelly pulled me aside and said, "Look, you're not doing us any good here. I'm going to send you home." I hadn't shed any tears since I started the interferon shots, but I'd reached a terminal point. I felt defeated. I felt broken and worn out like an abandoned toy. I so desperately wanted to defeat the virus absolutely and come through it polished and undamaged. I was trying hard to prove to Carol, to my family, to the public, and probably to myself that I was not going to be beaten by the disease and that I was going to go on with my life as usual. I saw for the first time that it was not going to happen that way. For the first time I buckled under and cried, not so much from the physical pain, but from the emotional strain.

Carol made an appointment to see doctors Nechtman and Fallon and told them, "He's at the bottom here. We need to do something." We went to see Dr. Nechtman first and Carl took a look at my nose and throat. I was blistered and raw. Carl explained that vocal chords are made up of voluntary and involuntary muscles and that you need more than six hours of sleep in order for the involuntary muscles to relax and heal themselves. By pushing myself in the hopes of keeping up appearances, I was actually doing more harm than good. I was in danger of doing permanent damage to my voice. Carl conducted a thorough round of tests and found no infection, but everything was inflamed.

We went on to Dr. Fallon, who did some blood work and thyroid work, checking the RNA and enzymes. My blood counts were well below normal, which explained the fatigue.

Carol and I were set for any news, though we prayed for the best. Dr. Fallon thought it important that we know that if the results of the test were poor—in other words, if the treatment was not yet effective—that there would not have been a reason to continue. If it wasn't working there wasn't a good alternative. Carol worried that I would have to start all over again a year later with possibly more liver damage, and longer recuperation. And Fallon warned that if it didn't respond very well the first time, there was a good chance that it would not respond at all.

I had reason for optimism. I could have again focused on the fact that I had acquired genotype two hepatitis C, which responded to therapy in an overwhelming majority of patients, as opposed to genotype one, for which there is a 48% success rate. But in truth I was not as enthusiastic about the possible results, good or bad. I was at a low point and determined to stay there.

It was Carol who got the call. Dr. Fallon informed us that the treatment was indeed working. As a result of the tests, Fallon told us that my enzymes were returning to normal levels and all signs pointed toward recovery. Carol prayed long and hard to thank God for the good news. It appeared that we were winning the battle. But the war was far from over. We had to continue the treatments until we could be sure that the infected cells would not regenerate. And so I knew what was ahead: 12 more treatments. 12 more weeks of misery. I tried to put the best face on it, and after a time I turned to radical means to take back a measure of control in my life.

Hair Today, Gone Tomorrow
I began to take a good look at myself in the mirror. It wasn't

a pretty sight. I'd cropped my hair close because it was falling out. One of my greatest fears was that I was going to look sick in public. Vanity is a sin, but it is also part of human nature. I refused to be pitied by strangers who might assume that I was hobbling toward the grave or that in fact I had just returned from one and was vacationing among the living. My vitality might have momentarily been taken away, but it was bound to return, and in the interim I wanted to feel stronger and take control of my body, even in the most symbolic of ways. As my hair continued to thin, and as the patches of scalp began to show through, I made a decision.

I went in to work to discuss with both Garry and Roy the possibility of shaving my head. In fact, by this time it had become more than a possibility. I had decided upon it. I wanted to feel them out and include them in the decision since my image would drastically change and they were responsible for selling my image to advertisers as part of the news team. They supported me and I went home prepared to say goodbye to the bald patches, the eyebrows falling into my plate, and the sink full of hair.

I was more than halfway through the hepatitis C therapy. The decision to go bald was empowering and I came home to tell Carol and the kids. I wasn't expecting that my looks would improve, because there's probably nothing less attractive than a short, chubby, bald, white guy undergoing chemo. But it was my emotional state that would be most drastically uplifted, and that meant more to me than my image in the mirror.

We gathered the kids together after dinner that night and had what we called a shaving party. We borrowed clippers from a friend who cuts our hair and went to the back deck with a stool and towel.

The children were in a bit of shock when they realized what we were doing. When first asked if they wanted to help shave their daddy bald, they'd all responded with an enthusiastic, "Yeah!" But when it was time, they couldn't believe I was actually going to do it. So I let each one of them have a turn using the clippers to cut it off. It wasn't much work since there was so little left, but we turned it into a game for them and it was strangely relaxing for me. It was my way of sharing the experience with them, allowing them to contribute to my recovery, perhaps a way to retrieve some of that time I'd lost when I'd unintentionally pushed them away.

After I was well shaved, I went in to remove the leftover stubble. The children spent a good thirty minutes rubbing daddy's smooth new chrome dome. I went to the mirror after we were finished. My head gleamed in the bathroom light, a badge of honor and a testament to the power of positive thinking. I felt like I had beaten this horrific disease already by taking my hair away before hepatitis C could do it for me. Unfortunately, the sense of well-being would not last.

Wanting to Quit

The effects of therapy are not always consistent. Patients can expect periods of relative ease or reduced discomfort. But at any moment the nausea, the dizziness, the fevers, and all of the other symptoms associated with treatment can return in the most debilitating way imaginable. That's what happened to me in the fifth month. I had a month left of treatment and I could barely walk. Every dreaded side effect returned with a vengeance, as if taking a last stand. The virus seemed to know that I was soon planning to show it the door.

The negative voices I'd managed to momentarily keep at bay spoke to me again. "We've gone through enough, haven't we?" my alter ego said. "Five months of therapy, and look at us! Bags under our eyes, eyebrows gone, bald, nausea all the time, snapping at Carol and the kids, losing our faith. We can't even make it to church because we're doubled over the toilet on Sundays like clockwork." I had to agree

I had hit a wall. I was tired and I was done. I couldn't take anymore. I was not only in pain; I was embarrassed, I was frustrated, and I was scared. Yes, scared. What if I couldn't make it all the way and get rid of this? I would likely die from it. And I wouldn't die quickly. It would take years, slowly robbing me of my health until some doctor, perhaps Fallon, would look at me disapprovingly over his glasses. "I told you this would happen," he would say before he announced my impending doom. Would I see my kids grow up? Would I walk Madison and Trinity down the aisle? Would I watch my son pitch from a major league mound? I had to fight through it; I had so much to live for. But, over time, that strength weakened and I was ready to give in. I had been through enough. The dark voices convinced me that it was time to move on past the self-inflicted agony and take my chances.

I had a doctor's appointment with Fallon and headed in with Carol and my son Fowler. For months I had managed to convince myself that nothing, especially a microscopic organism, was going to beat me. But hepatitis C had persuaded me over the long course of trying to rid myself of it, that it was stronger, more determined, and better armed. To prove how crazy the experience was making me, I also held the exact opposite opinion that perhaps I'd actually done enough to win. The virus had been beating me up, but it had taken a good licking—five months of weekly injections and popping pills and blood work once a month. It had shown signs of weakening. Maybe I didn't have to fight back anymore. Maybe I'd killed it off, or if I was lucky the silent killer was limping so badly that it would never make it to the finish line. I was clearly looking for an excuse.

Fallon walked in to the office. I was sitting on the examining table. He did the routine abdominal push, and checked me over. I let him go through the motions, trying to decide when to ask him what had been lingering in my mind. After he sat down, I let it out. "Man, I want to quit." He looked at me, seeing immediately that I was serious.

"Mark," he said, "you have invested a huge amount of time and energy up to this point and you're having bad side effects. But we need to look at the big picture. You are responding to treatment." He was right, but then he was approaching it from the outside. Almost anyone can rationalize necessary pain as long as it's not his own.

I wanted to say that it was more than the physical discomfort. I wasn't able to do my job. I wanted to admit that I sometimes sagged against the weather wall in the studio during my forecasts because it was the only thing keeping me up. My mind was so scattered by then that I couldn't come up with enough things to say to fill out my time slot on air. I'd forget names of places or lose my train of thought, and even when that train was moving at top speed,

it felt like it had a cargo full of ballast, slowing my reac-
tions, dulling my wit. Sometimes, frankly, I felt like an
incompetent jerk on the air. That was hard to take, because
I have always had pride in my work. If my work suffered,
then I was no longer a professional. I was just a victim of a
shameless, unrelenting disease.

I wanted to say that I had been abused so badly by the
virus that I was passing that abuse along to the only people
who mattered to me. I wanted that person to go far away
and never return. I wanted it to be over. I was five months
in, with only one month to go, but four weeks...good Lord.
Those weeks seemed to stretch out before me like a barren
desert terrain with no oasis on the horizon. I couldn't do it
anymore.

Fallon stepped up his pitch. "Mark, this is six months
of your life, you've committed to it, it's working. You've
just got to pick the things in your life that are important to
you, and do what you can do to be around for the next
thirty years to raise your kids properly and have those ten
years to apologize to your wife. At some point you have to
stop saying *woe is me* and take the dang treatment and
tough it through. And if you've got to stink at your job for
a few months, you've got to leave your pride at the door
and look at the big picture."

I sat and sighed. He made sense. He always made sense.
I wondered how he did it. But when a man decides he's tired
of catching a beating there's almost nothing you can say to
lift him off the canvas. He either gets up on his own two legs
or he's carried out of the ring. I said, "I don't think I can."

I wasn't proud of my decision. In my head I was shout-
ing every insult I could imagine, all of it directed squarely at

the guy on the examination table. Finally, Mr. Invincible had thrown in the towel. I accepted that I had been defeated by a creature I had never even seen with my own eyes, an invisible assassin. I kept yelling inside, "You coward. You are a coward! You quitter! I thought you were stronger than that. You're nothing if you quit this!"

Where was my faith? Where was my belief that God would help me endure? God seemed distant, unable to see me through. I believed that it was up to me to face the pain and I knew I wasn't going to be up to the task. That voice I was hearing was a manifestation of a hurt and scared child growing up with insecurities. I would remind myself of this when I was ready to quit anything.

No one else knew what was ringing inside my bald skull. Fallon simply said, "Well, okay. I'll let you quit." I was stunned. Why wasn't he talking me out of it? "I'll tell you what," he added, "go home and think about it. If you decide then that you want to quit treatments, then you can. The only thing you owe me though is a phone call. Fair enough?"

"Fair enough," I said, and began gathering my things to leave. Carol was helping my son Fowler stand because his legs were still wobbly. Fallon looked over to the two of them and said, "You know, he looks just like you!"

More than anything he could have said to me at that moment, it was that observation that put everything in perspective for me. Fowler did look like me. If I raised him right, he might even act like me and respect me. I love my son. I refused to set a poor example. Would Fowler one day face a crucial decision, follow my lead, and quit? It was a stretch, I know, to project my fears so far into the future.

He would in all likelihood never remember this visit to Dr. Fallon nor my decision to bow out ungracefully. But how would the story be told in the years to come? How would I explain it to him? I smiled and bowed my head. "Okay, you win. You're right. I won't quit."

Sometimes, when you look hard enough, you can catch God winking at you. I'd asked where He was and He answered. "Trust in the LORD with all your heart," Proverbs 3:5 advises, "and lean not on your own understanding; in all your ways acknowledge Him, and He shall direct your paths" (NKJV).

Time Out

I needed a respite from the Grim Reaper, who seemed to have been hanging around, scratching at my civility with his bony claws and influencing me with his poor attitude. The soul can bear enormous strain if God is allowed to work miracles within you, but I felt like even the Lord had called for a time out. So when the opportunity came to travel and indulge in my favorite pastime, I took it.

As a precaution, Carol wrote down our home phone number and made me take it along. By this time in the therapy my memory was full of holes and even common things like names and addresses escaped me.

I was not happy with my looks. I was frighteningly pale, and now bald. But when I decided to go see a dear friend of mine, Todd Jones, a relief pitcher for the Colorado Rockies, I decided to take it in stride. I wasn't given much of a choice.

Search any male professional sports team and you will be hard pressed to find political correctness much in evidence. A few examples: upon seeing me, and throughout the visit to training sessions, I was greeted variously by, "Dude, you've got to get some sun," "Work on the tan while you're here. Go hatless!" and "Dude, you're really white!" I thanked Todd for the reminders.

During one practice, I was standing by the fence nearest first base. Taking Jones' advice I had taken my hat off to get some sun. I was whiter than the snow in which I had concealed my wife's engagement ring.

More than a few Rockies took notice of me while jogging between the foul line and center field. Unaware I was causing such a spectacle, I was surprised to hear outfielder Larry Walker's deep, booming voice. "You know," he said, "from a distance, it kind of looks like a latex glove!" I had to give him that one. I literally laughed out loud. Then designated hitter Gabe Kapler suggested that I find a tanning bed, fast. I took the ribbing with pleasure from some outstanding players for whom I held great respect. Larry followed up the first with another. "Dude, it's blinding when you get real close!"

Jones and some of the other pitchers came back to greet me as the practice was wrapping up. I told him about the beating I had taken on the sidelines. He agreed that I'd been at the short end of some very funny put downs, but as we headed to the clubhouse in their spring training stadium we ran into Larry Walker. Todd stopped, gestured at me, and said, "Hey, Walker, what's up with messing with my boy who's dying on chemo? I mean, you hammered him, with only 3 weeks left to live!"

Walker froze, every ounce of blood draining from his face. I tried to maintain my composure, but it didn't hold for long, and as Larry Walker caught me smiling he broke up laughing.

It was just what I needed. I'd been living under a cloud for six months, trying to hold the center together. Much of who I was and what I'd known had been shaken to the core of my being. Over the course of the treatments I was forced to reexamine my values and my beliefs. Such weighty issues do not lend themselves to humor. The visit to the Rockies' training camp helped me put some of it into perspective and reminded me that humor can often be the best form of medicine. I breathed in the arid, Arizona air, listened to the slap of baseballs hitting leather mitts and the cracks of bats sending baseballs into the azure sky. I applied the sound of laughter to my bruised ego like a balm, and a sense of balance returned. God, not the disease, was in control of my life. Hepatitis C may have held dominion over my body for a time, but one does not define oneself by his or her physical shell, but rather the spiritual being the corporeal shell houses. Both the body and the spirit belong to the Lord in any case, as put forth in 1 Corinthians 6:19 (NKJV): "Or do you not know that your body is the temple of the Holy Spirit who is in you, whom you have from God, and you are not your own?" I trusted in God to deliver me.

Chapter Seven
Clearing Skies

There is a popular optical illusion often found in puzzle books depicting the profile of a withered old crone with a prominent nose; seen in a different way it is a beautiful young woman wearing a heavy fox stole. You could look at this picture for hours on end and switch between the two interpretations at will, each seeming as undeniably clear as the other. It's all in how you see it. That is the magic of perception.

When Carol and I were approaching my twenty-fourth and final interferon injection, we experienced a similar trick of perception. She saw an end to a long journey. She had literally counted the number of injections from the first to the twelfth and down to the last. Over the course of the final weeks of therapy the joy of anticipation dawned in her eyes like a child at the beginning of the holiday season.

I admit that it had to have been hard on her. When you know someone's soul as well as I know Carol's, even little differences leave their mark. I can look at her now and see the innumerable humiliations I must have inflicted upon her, the ones I have since forgotten as the therapy robbed me of so many of my memories. There is nothing in the way of an accusation in her eyes, but she was clearly wounded, and in conversations about our trials together her eyes hold the promise of tears. "Your mother and I spent many hours on the phone, crying," she has said.

To Carol, who held the family together as I threatened to tear it apart for six months, the final shot was the payoff. It was the last time, she said, that she would ever have to make me sick, the last time she would ever watch me struggle for breath, or see me fall to my knees in agony and feel that she was to blame. It was the end of the duality that she was making me better by trying to kill me.

She therefore conducted the last treatment as a ceremony, laying out the instruments and the medicine the way a host lays out the good china. It was significant to her and she treated it as such. She saw the beautiful young woman in the optical illusion.

I, on the other hand, was staring plainly at the old crone. I remember the last four to five weeks being the hardest for me, not just physically, but also because well-wishers would approach and try with the best of intentions to cheer me up. "Hey, buddy, you've only got five more to go," or, "Chin up, Mark, just four more." "Wow, man, three left and you're home free." I smiled and thanked them graciously, but I fought like heck the urge to spit back at them, "Yeah, sure! Why don't you try three of these? Try just one!" I was sure no one would take me up on my offer.

I saw my immediate future laid out before me: another

round of nausea, lightheaded dashes to the bathroom, the firebrands of pain in my knees, the headaches, the lapses of reason, the alertness of a sleepwalker, feeling as if God was taking the ground beneath my feet and the very air around me and shaking it like a snow globe. By the last treatment tests showed that I was 2 1/2 pints low on blood. (Three pints low and you can be approved for a certain medication to help bring the blood counts up. But shy of three you'll likely end up in a battle with your insurance company. This is what our doctors told us, and there is some long, drawn-out explanation behind it that you might be willing to explore with your physician if it ever comes up, but in short it meant I would have to live with it.) To me, the week leading up to the last injection was no different than any other. I approached it with the same feeling of dread, my disposition sinking as we progressed toward every Friday. My mood did not influence Carol's, however, and she gratefully thanked God for carrying us through to the end.

By the final treatment I felt like a human pincushion. I had refused to change the injection site, though I had the option to have Carol administer the interferon in my stomach or my inner thigh in addition to my arm. I stuck with my arm, if you will pardon the pun, based on the reasoning that I would rather put as few body parts as possible through the wringer. My arm was horribly swollen and red and so inflamed it barely felt like flesh. Carol's attempt to pinch the fat of the arm at the injection site had been abandoned long ago, since pinching equaled pain. At my bitter insistence that she just get it over with, she sank the needle into my arm for the last time.

Withdrawal

Perception was again toying with us. For all the emphasis Carol had put on the finality of the event, hepatitis C was not finished with us yet. The therapy, more severe than the symptoms of the disease, had ruled our every action for months and now it did not seem to wish to let us go on our way, like a rude party guest lingering long after his hosts have succumbed to exhaustion.

According to Mike Fallon, my body had been the receptacle for so many drugs that I would not detoxify for at least three to six months. I had had my clock cleaned by a vicious opponent and he wisely advised me not to make any major plans or to expect a swift recovery. In fact, in a clandestine conversation he told Carol to expect things to get worse before they got better. I had put poisons in my body, and I had done so for so long that my body now expected them, craved them in fact. I literally suffered withdrawal symptoms. For several months my body was at war, exorcising the twin demons of the disease and the therapy. I remained on prescribed narcotics to dull the pain, but I was so desperate to get my body clean I tried to wean myself off of them quickly, despite Fallon's advice that we proceed with caution. I paid for my impatience in spades. In its cry for interferon and ribavirin, my body amplified every sound, every smell until I felt like screaming at every touch and every whisper. Just when Carol and the rest of the family believed that they would have me back, I let my anger fly.

Once during this period my mother came over to visit. I think she must have been there for Carol and the kids as much as she was there for me because I remained in a foul mood and I was handing out abuse in equal measures to all, though I was continuing to give Carol an especially hard time, as quick-tempered and harsh as I had ever been during therapy, probably more so. The strain of it began to show on her face. As a family we were dealing with a lot of serious issues at once; among them, my older brother Rich had just suffered a heart attack and his marriage was failing.

On the way to the hospital in Montgomery I became increasingly angry at my brother's wife. She was of course at the hospital and I became so enraged that I nearly had to be restrained. It took quite awhile for other family members to calm me down enough so that she and I could remain in the same room. My mother witnessed this with the keen observation of a parent and if she disapproved she said nothing about it. But I discovered later that she was also watching Carol closely and had seen the hurt expression that my wife was beginning to wear daily. Throughout the treatment my mom became Carol's confidante. Because of my frequent memory loss, she knew better than I what I was putting my wife through.

My mother came back to Birmingham to keep us company and saw firsthand what she had heard Carol explain to her often, crying over the phone. I snapped at the kids and I said some very hurtful things to my wife. After dinner the family retired to the television room and I continued acting out and criticizing Carol. I went too far. Finally, Carol's patience wore out and she left the room, followed soon after by my mom. Mom went upstairs and sat on the porch alone. I found her there very distraught.

"What's wrong, Mom?" I asked, honestly unaware of the havoc I had wreaked throughout the day.

"Do you really want to know?" she said.

"Yes."

"Well, you better go get me some tissues, then," she said.

"Are you kidding?" I asked.

"No, Mark. I'm going to need some tissues."

When I returned with the tissues, my mother asked me to sit down and let me have it. "I have had enough of you being hateful and angry. At the hospital you don't think we knew but we could see that you had said something awful to Carol. I'm tired of you treating her so badly when she's done so much for you. You've got a wonderful girl in there who loves you with everything she has. She helps you, does more for you than you could ever ask, and look how you treat her."

I should have heard what she was telling me, but all I could think of was the amount of nerve it took to insult me the way she did in my own house. My house!

My mom was crying now, her emotions getting away from her. She'd only tore into me once before like this and we hadn't spoken for three months afterwards as a result. "You're being hurtful," she said. "I'm sick of it, your wife is sick of it, and your brothers and sisters are sick of it. You have so many great things to offer. Your children adore you. Your family adores you. I raised you to help people, not hurt them."

Seeing your mother in tears over something you've said or done is sobering, and I knew she was right. My mother believed that no one had spoken honestly to me about my behavior and thought that it was time that I heard the truth.

I stopped to consider what she said to me and I finally relented. I offered an olive branch. "Well," I said, "why don't you come back downstairs with us?" My mom stayed the night and I tried to keep my anger in check, knowing that I owed everyone a round of apologies.

Thankfully, there was a measure of good news to be found in the immediate aftermath of my last treatment. I was told that my blood count was coming back up. My iron level was on the rise just ten days after the interferon shot. My body was healing, though I overestimated the speed at which I was recovering. Approximately six weeks after the shot I was invited to play in a charity softball game. I took it as an opportunity to prove that I was back on top, that I had not been beaten as severely as it had appeared. It was important to me to show anyone who had bothered to watch my journey through treatment that I was a winner who could take on all challengers. Carol and the most sensible among my friends, that is to say almost all of them, told me that I didn't need to prove anything to anyone and that I should be taking it easy. True to form I insisted that I was going to play and no one could tell me otherwise. I insisted so forcefully that Carol and I had an argument about it. Now armed with the gee-whiz common sense that accompanies hindsight, I probably should have thrown in the towel. Up at bat, I took a swing, connected, and took off in a full sprint toward first base. Somewhere between first base and the dugout I thought, "I'm not going to make it." This revelation was bolstered somewhat by the fact that my lungs were trying to climb out of my chest. I pushed myself harder at top speed and my knees, my ankles, and every limb begged me to stop. My heart sank a little at the realization that even at more than a month past therapy I remained as weak as an infant. After that I halfheartedly played the outfield and stopped swinging for the fences because I didn't want to accidentally knock it out of the park and be forced to run for home.

The whole experience left a bitter taste in my mouth. For all that I had put my family through, and for all of the pain and emotional distress I suffered, I remained in the grip of the side effects of hepatitis C therapy. My family again caught the brunt of my anger. During one phone conversation with my mother I let my frustration get the best of me and I berated her furiously. Thankfully, this woman who had given me life and whom I adore more than any woman other than my wife understood that I was again reacting to the drugs in my bloodstream. She accepted it as a temporary stage as parents so often accept the unruliness of their children, expecting that it would pass and that her son would return in short order.

But it seemed an eternity to me, the nights endless. Sleep did not come easily, and I took to sitting alone in the television room downstairs, the place I went to receive treatments for so many months. I took refuge in the music I played on my computer in the dark, and Carol would often sit in the chair opposite mine, a loving presence. When I found a song I liked I would sit back and close my eyes, letting the music take my hand and walk me to a better place. I could listen to music for hours in the darkness with Carol by my side. I could leave behind all of my cares and drift to a brighter, happier place, which is what God intends when we pray. He encourages us to slow down and take stock of our blessings when too often we see only the things that hasten us along. I had to learn to be still and learn to let go and live.

Life of the Party

I was content to pray and thank God for all of His mercies, for living through me and Carol and my friends and family when we so urgently needed Him. I had no intentions to celebrate our good fortune, but my wife had other plans.

Just a week after we wrapped up therapy, on the first Friday in six months when I wasn't scheduled to poison myself, Carol put together what we later came to see as a "life party." It had been long in planning, which came as a surprise since I had joked that no one could put one over on me. Surprise parties never came as a surprise, and so when Scott Dawson picked me up to attend a meeting that day, I suspected nothing.

During the months preceding the discovery of my illness, Scott, a popular evangelist and author, become a very close friend. He had contracted hepatitis A and with a sympathetic eye I watched him battle the disease. Scott was among the first people I entrusted with news of my discovery. Because of his experiences with hepatitis he knew what I was going through and he became a true spiritual advisor, a companion, and a trusted confidant.

On that Friday after my last treatment Scott said that we needed to tie up some loose ends in preparation for a fundraiser to be held at the Hoover Met (home of the Birmingham Barons, the team where Michael Jordan garnered so much press in his quest to become a baseball player). We were preparing for Safe at Home, for which we roll out the red carpet in an all-encompassing ministry at the stadium for people who have not yet been saved. We invite church members and buy tickets for those who can't afford them and bring the masses to Jesus Christ—a worthy cause. I was glad to be a part of it, but at the time I was still in the clutches of the interferon. Scott drove us to the meeting, and I believe steam must have come out of my ears when I found that of all the people scheduled to attend, only a few actually showed.

On our way back through the Magic City, Scott turned to me and said, "Listen, I've got to run by the golf club for a minute." He claimed that he needed to go by and drop something off. But I was not feeling well. All I could think of was home and I asked him to drop me off first.

"It's only going to take two minutes," he said. "I've just got to drop this thing off."

"I'd really rather you take me home," I said.

Scott agreed, but not without taking one last stab at his assigned mission to bring me to the clubhouse. This time when he asked me to take the ride with him, I backed off in deference to our friendship. If he really needed to go by the clubhouse, then it was only a few minutes from home and it wasn't worth losing my temper at Scott, who was doing so much for so many people.

We arrived in the parking lot of the clubhouse at around 5:30 in the evening and I immediately noticed that it was literally packed with cars. Bitterly, I thought of the time and effort it would take Scott to locate the person he had come to meet, but I agreed to go along with him since anything was better than sitting and waiting in the car.

Walking past the cars I remember seeing someone trotting by and I was struck with a faint flash of recognition. It sure looked like Mark Congleton from WDJC. I mentioned it to Scott as we entered the lobby and his feigned nonchalance should be studied by budding actors everywhere.

"Hmmm, that's interesting," he said unconvincingly. He opened the door to the clubhouse with a theatrical flourish and suddenly a great mass of people screamed, "Surprise." I was absolutely floored. I'd been taken. I walked in and a hush settled over the room, smiles still in place. "What are y'all doing here?" I asked. My mom came over and grabbed me in a big hug. "I'm very proud of you," she said. "You made it. You did it. I love you so much." I thanked her and hugged her back. I was in for another surprise. Carol, who saw me at the door, disappeared into the clubhouse kitchen. She returned with familiar faces in tow. Tom Castilla—"the Big Flip" we call him because he's half American, half Filipino—is a friend from college. There he was with his wife all the way from Pensacola, Florida. He gave me a big bear hug. Melissa and Shubert Chang came from Miami. Good friends Scott and Mary Beth Johnson came from Lakeland, Florida, John McDaniel and his wife had driven in from my hometown, Prattville. Coworkers like Latrish Williford, Andrew Wyatt, Christopher Sign, Dave Baird, Pam Huff, Keisa Sharpe, and Chris Osborne also showed. Among them were others who had been at the receiving end of some terrible tantrums while I was undergoing treatment. Jeremy King, a producer, was one of them.

Jeremy was at the helm of the show on a day I was not feeling my best. My first appearance on the air during the show is what we call first weather, a brief introduction to the weather segment to come later in the broadcast. I was already at the weather wall ready to deliver the tease, while Jeremy kept pushing story after story ahead of me. At some point you simply run out of time and you're forced to go to a commercial break. I've never been good at standing by.

I'm either on or I'm not. I drilled him over the intercom. "I can't believe I'm out here waiting; I've got other things to do," I remember telling him. "We'll get to you, just hang on," he said. I was steamed. "Are we going to do first weather, are we going to forget about it, or what?" I was nearly yelling while the show continued. "You're just rolling your eyes at us," Jeremy said, frustrated. Then I lost it. I actually told him to just shut up. I never apologized. And there he was at the party, like it had never happened, offering me his sincerest congratulations. I was dumbfounded.

I looked over to another pair of friends and for a moment I couldn't believe what I was seeing. One of them, my next-door neighbor, was associated with a financial scandal in a major southeastern healthcare company. As I write this, he is currently in prison. The other was the federal agent responsible for his arrest. They were both at the party. By then the investigation was in full swing and they were both aware of their respective roles, my one friend as the suspect in a federal investigation, the other as the representative of the government nearly ready to close the case against him. I remember seeing both of them shaking hands. They both turned as I approached. They had momentarily put the investigation aside, had even called each other and said, hey look, this is a big deal for Mark and it's more important that we do this. We're both going to be there, let's help him enjoy it. What incredible people. Under normal circumstances the two of them would not even be in the same room.

I looked around at the guests. They were old, young, black, white, Filipino, Chinese, short, tall, and all of them beautiful for what they had done for me.

It was a large party and I could not have hoped to speak to each and every guest, but I wanted to do so. Each had gone out of their way to support me and had asked for nothing in return. I reached out to as many of them as I could, remembering that they had prayed for me all along.

I said once before that churches put me on their prayer lists. It had been easy to accept those prayers with detached thanks. It was the same with people finding me on the street to wish me well, or callers who left uplifting messages on my voice mail. The sheer number of offers of support was overwhelming.

One woman sent me a card with a $30 check enclosed. She wrote that she didn't have much but that she wanted me to have the check to take my family out to dinner, to leave my cares behind for just one night. She was a widow living on her own in the country, somewhere in northwest Alabama, and she wrote that the gift was the only way she knew to help. I sent her back a note with the same check enclosed, and wrote that it meant more to me than she realized, but that I couldn't accept it because God had already blessed me with the resources to take care of my family. I suggested that she might donate the money to the American Liver Foundation or any other charity of her choosing.

I was touched, but I don't believe I was able to understand it until I was standing amid a sea of friends, whose individual outpouring of warmth put it all in perspective. It took the generosity of my closest friends and colleagues to see that each prayer was a gift from the heart. The widow's gift was like the poor widow in Scripture who gave two small copper coins to the treasury. Jesus watched as the rich also contributed their portion. But it was the widow, Jesus said, who "put in more than all; for all these out of their abundance have put in offerings for God, but she out of her poverty put in all the livelihood that she had" (Luke 21:3–4 NKJV). The woman who sent me the check had probably sent more than she could afford, and for that I will be eternally grateful.

Every one of those thousand or so e-mails and each of those hundreds of letters that I'd kept represented a kindhearted person. I suddenly saw them as individuals with their own concerns who had taken time out of their busy lives to connect with me, and offer me a light out of the darkness. Yes, they dealt with unruly children or emotionally disconnected husbands or wives, or late bills, or homes where crumbs lay scattered across the floor. But they found the time to say, "God bless you and keep you. May God give you strength in your time of need." The power of that single epiphany nearly brought me to tears.

The party was a huge success. Guests took turns roasting me, which turned out to be surprisingly easy to do since I had given all of them such ample material in the last year. A musician friend of mine put on a great show. Another friend who is an Elvis impersonator arrived in his full Las Vegas regalia with the hair and the glasses and gaudy rings, and he performed three songs. Then it was my chance to speak and I just fell apart. I barely remember what I said beyond "Thanks."

I looked at pictures of the party a week later, when I'd had a chance to reflect on what it meant to me. I saw a room full of people who had nothing to gain by showing their support. It did not make them richer. It hadn't secured their jobs or guaranteed them any special considerations. I felt blessed to have had such unselfish people in my life. God put these friends in my path to help see me through a tremendous hardship.

Test Results

In some ways I'd survived and triumphed in the battle against the disease, but in no way did I believe that I had won the war. Though I'd been making steady progress toward recovery throughout my therapy, I was aware of the small percentage of patients with genotype 2 hepatitis C for whom interferon and ribavirin treatments are not effective. I knew I could be included in that percentage and it was a frightening prospect. What if after all I had been through and after all the heartache I'd caused I still wasn't clear of the virus? What would my options be? The picture could have appeared very grim. But despite my best efforts to the contrary, the seed of optimism was growing in my mind as we approached the hepatitis C RNA check three months after my final treatment. It would be a simple procedure: I would have blood drawn as I have countless times since the discovery of the virus and a laboratory would check for the presence of the virus's RNA. If it failed to show, that was great. I would be in the clear. If it did show then I would be back to square one, the worst possible scenario.

While I was still undergoing therapy I treated tests like these with nonchalance at best, and at worst, contempt. No matter what the results, I knew I would soon have to return to the horror of interferon injections and all of its crippling side effects. This time would be different. There were no injections to contemplate, no sideshow of disorientation and sleeplessness, no nausea, no voices in my head encouraging the worst of my behavior. Even so I strove to maintain an even keel. Alexander Pope wrote, "Blessed is he who expects nothing, for he shall never be disappointed."

My forced pessimism was in place as I got the blood drawn at UAB. I sat in Dr. Fallon's office as a hundred things ran through my mind, hope playing against fear. When Mike came in he was jovial as usual, consistent with every other visit to his office, but he seemed to have an extra bounce in his step. I suspected that he knew something that I didn't and that in the best scenario he was happy not to have to deliver bad news. As my physician, Mike was well aware of the difficult process of therapy and I think it would have pained him to tell me and Carol he'd been forced to put us through hell for nothing.

As it turns out, he did not have any news, good or bad. He sat at his desk and attempted to pull up the results of the blood test on his computer, but apparently the results had not been posted to my records and we left in a heightened state of anxiety.

Mike reassured us that results would come in a day or so, and I could not think of a worse way to spend a day. I went to work and I decided to force myself not to think about it at all, which I thought was a fine plan until the phone rang. Friends and family called repeatedly to check on me. "Hey man, you're done. Aren't you excited?" they would invariably say. Maintaining a healthy cynicism, I would dryly reply. "Yes. I'm thrilled." I was not about to celebrate ahead of schedule.

I was lying on my bed at home, exhausted from just a few hours at work, but still awake when Carol walked in the room. She was beaming and wore an expression I hadn't seen on her face in more months that I cared to remember. There was a light in her eyes, a childlike glow.

"I got a call today," she said.

In a prone position facing our TV, I mumbled, "Oh, really? Great. From who?"

She smiled. "Doctor Fallon's office called. Your blood work is perfect. You're cured, baby! You're cured!"

She did not get the reaction she was hoping for. I don't think I even sat up. "Really?" I said. "That's good."

It was as if I'd thrown water on her torch and drenched her in the process. "That's good? What do you mean that's good? That's great news! I figured you'd be so excited to hear about it!"

I couldn't explain to her then and I can't explain now why I felt so unaffected at that moment. It was cause for celebration, and if anyone ever put this story on film I might request that the scene be reconstructed to include flying doves, a marching band, hundreds of brightly colored balloons, and confetti and party favors. But at the time I was emotionally spent. All of my strength had been expended in the fight against the disease and I can only assume that I had nothing left with which to celebrate. All I wanted to do was to pick myself up off the floor and return to a normal routine, to prove that I had in fact beaten the disease and that it hadn't taken my life or my ability to work. Looking in the mirror I still saw the pale, nearly bald little man with no eyebrows who still gasped for air going up a flight of stairs.

Still incredulous, Carol came to me time and again expressing her disbelief that I wasn't soaring through the clouds. "I can't believe you're not excited. Your count is good. The virus is gone." I still felt nothing. It struck me as strange, but I poured my shallow pool of energy into work.

Becoming an Advocate

For months during therapy I resisted the role of advocate. I had traveled a road many people were about to travel or had traveled before, and a number of people reached out to me to ask for guidance: new hepatitis C patients, churches, civic groups, and schools, many of them wanting me to speak publicly about the disease and the brutal cure. But I was in no way ready to become the focus of a whirlwind of advocacy. First I had to heal, inside and out, and I wanted to take my time to do it. After I received the good news I began to take those calls. I knew I still had a long way to go in my journey toward full recovery, but the darkness was lifting and I believed it was time to raise the volume on this silent epidemic.

I began to speak at churches and in other venues. I had already established correspondence with many people through e-mail, but I went back through the messages, found their phone numbers, and called them to offer encouragement and to help them deal with what lay before them. I always hoped that during these conversations I would detail my experience with the disease and they would sincerely say something like, "That sounds horrible. But my treatment is going swimmingly. Can't say I've ever felt any of those symptoms. Tough break." It never worked out that way. Every one of them shared heartbreakingly similar tales of pain. I established a connection to them in this way, through the shared experience. I was again telling fortunes, only this time I needed no radar screens or sophisticated computer models. I knew what was ahead for them and they were eager for the knowledge as much as they were grateful for the human contact. They were able to teach me as well, as some of them had been unable to finish the full regimen of therapy. They'd quit before they were done. I'd been there and saw in them what could have easily been my fate if not for prayer, if not for Carol, Cole, Trinity, Madison, Fowler, Barbara Prater, and countless others. I helped wherever I could and I believe it saved me.

More than a week after we received the test results I sat alone in my room next to the garage where the family watches TV together. After everyone else retired for the night I chose some relaxing music and I gave myself time to reflect on my journey through hepatitis C, reliving all that I had seen, done, and felt. I saw all of my fears and faults magnified. I remembered where I had fallen and where I had risen and I recalled with wonder all the help I had been given in the rising. I saw how far God carried me. Each recollection dismantled the angry, dismissive walls I managed to build around myself and I was soon in tears. I had tears pouring down each cheek, one after another. I remember that as my chin fell to my chest and I started sobbing, I felt as if the release was cleansing my heart. I looked up to the ceiling tiles in the room, looking beyond the ceiling to heaven, and thanked God for the moment. Long in coming, I finally accepted that as a family we had won. I was cured. My body was still cleansing itself and I still felt remnants of anxiety and other side effects, but they were fading and the virus was dead and buried. I danced on its grave.

That night sparked a passion within me to share what I know. I was ready to be that advocate that I had avoided becoming for so long. I owed so much to so many people and though there was no way to repay them for what they had done for me, I knew that I could contribute to the well being of those who were lost and were looking for answers.

I am overwhelmed by the sheer number of people who come to me now for aid, and I welcome them. I don't always know their names or where they come from, and I am not often told more than I need to know about them, but I know enough. I know that I was once just like them. I spent a long time in the dark, cowering in fear of the unknown. Patients and caretakers, mothers and sisters and brothers and fathers, friends and confidants, and even neighbors of victims reach out to me in equal numbers. "We're scared," they say, "and we don't know who to turn to for help." I help them gladly, sparing no detail in the belief that being well-prepared is being well-armed. Hepatitis C may bring you to your knees, but it won't be able to sneak up on you if you know what's coming.

What I would have given for advance knowledge of exactly what to expect in the fight against hepatitis C. It is why I wrote this book, so that a multitude of patients and everyone around them affected by the disease could use my experiences as a beacon of hope.

The Still, Small Voice

Three months after the charity softball game during which I'd run out of steam halfway to first base, my body and my mind hoisted their white flags in the air, signaling a truce in the war that had been raging between them. I was no longer clamoring for painkillers or interferon. For the first time in nearly a year I began to see things more clearly, and

I concluded that since I was healing well it was time to begin to heal the thing I cherished most: my relationship with the family I loved. I still suffered through ticks and quirks and anxieties that swirled around me like ghosts, but I sensed they were fading like shadows chased before the dawn.

At my most lucid moment I decided that the Prater family deserved a break. I told Carol that in appreciation for everything that she had done for me I would take her and the kids anywhere she wanted to go on vacation. She wasn't interested in a cruise and I'm not a big fan of the beach, but Carol had never been out west. We browsed the Internet for possible getaway locations and narrowed it down to destinations that were remote, with no lines for attractions, no scheduled itineraries, no guided tours, no phones, no faxes, no computers with Internet access. Places like this still exist, though judging by the number of choices we found, they are shrinking in number. We wanted to step away from the world for a little while and focus on the family.

We settled on Montana and a rustic cabin by the Yellowstone River. Dr. Fallon had only recently weaned me off pain medication and, still feeling the last vestiges of therapy-induced anxiety, I did not enjoy the flight out west. But I felt my concerns lifting with each mile away from home.

The destination was everything we could have hoped for. I stood and listened to the babbling river, I held my breath to hear the whistling wind, I bathed in the sight of the glorious, snow-capped mountain range beyond the trees, physically and spiritually miles away from the ordinary troubles of the world. You could not stand in the presence of this flawless scenery and doubt its divine creation. I did not find comfort in the silence of this pristine place, but in the absence of silence, in the spiritual chorus of calming waters and blindingly bright blue skies.

In 1 Kings 19:11–13, the prophet Elijah is on the mount in the wilderness. He fled to the wilderness because the king of Israel, Ahab, sought his death. Elijah had been a mighty warrior for God and he came to be discouraged. In this place in the wilderness he encountered God. God spoke, encouraging His saint to be still. "And he said, Go forth, and stand upon the mount before the LORD. And, behold, the LORD passed by, and a great and strong wind rent the mountains, and brake in pieces the rocks before the LORD; but the LORD was not in the wind: and after the wind an earthquake; but the LORD was not in the earthquake: and after the earthquake a fire; but the LORD was not in the fire: and after the fire a still small voice."

During therapy I tried to convince myself that I was weak and alone. I directed my anger at my family, my friends, my coworkers, and God. These voices howled and raged and left me broken. But in the quiet of Montana I was made whole again. *You are not alone*, a still small voice said. *You are not weak. I was with you all along, through the crashes of thunder and torrents of rain, through the buffeting winds I sent you blessings and should you be still, you will see them.* That comforting voice, God's voice, restored my spirit, for I knew He had seen me through the silent storm.

Box of Blessings

I heard a story of a man who went to heaven. An angel greeted him and took him through a large building filled floor-to-ceiling with boxes. All of the boxes had names on them and the angel led the man to his box. It was large and unopened. The man asked if he could open it and the angel replied, "No, you can't." The man asked why not. The angel replied that the box was full of the blessings that God had given him but which he had never accepted as his own—gifts that God had bestowed upon him that he had never used in life. These gifts were of no use after the man's life on earth had come to an end. Therefore the box would remain closed, a reminder of a life unfulfilled.

I hope that when the angel leads me through to heaven, that sorrowful building will hold no unopened boxes for me. I have been blessed with a family whom I can now never take for granted. I have been blessed with a career that allows me to care for those I love—a means to an end, not an end in itself. I have been blessed with proper perspective that tells me it doesn't matter how successful I am or how many cars I can squeeze into my garage or how much money I can make or how big a house I can buy. Yes, I'm still human, and subject to the whimsies of human nature. I can still be argumentative and quirky, but I recognize when I have gone too far. Proverbs 24:16 says that "a righteous man may fall seven times and rise again." Seven times. I passed that mark long ago. But I rise, and upon each rising become more of the man God wants me to be.

I cherish my children. Now that I am physically capable, I jump on the trampoline, I hit baseballs in the batting cage, I watch movies with them on the big screen TV, I take them fishing and hunting. A year and a half ago, my kids would ask, "Dad, can we go fishing today?" I may have been working since 3:30 in the morning. I used to say, "No,

I've got other stuff to do. Get your momma to take you over there." I still have other stuff to do, but I have risen and I will now say, "Yeah, let's go for an hour." Time is a blessing. I would give anything to get back the time I lost with my family. I'm trying to make up for it. I learned what God had been trying to tell me all this time.

I cherish my wife. Carol is my rock, and through this experience with hepatitis C I have seen more of her true self than I ever have before. Now that I am well, and given the chance to reflect on the experience, I see every hardship she endured and I don't have the words to tell her how much she means to me. Our marriage has never been stronger. God never let her quit on me, though I gave her more than a few excuses to run away and leave me to grouse at my reflection. I owe her my life and my eternal love.

What I Read in the Skies

When I look up into the sky now I no longer look for my father's bird. I can still see the shape of things to come in the physical realm: a storm cloud on the horizon, the strong gust of wind holding the promise of rain. But now I see other things. I see the divine complexity of God's plan, the comedy and the tragedy of my purpose through His will; I see that all things are meant to be and that some journeys have a beginning but not an end. I'm still taking this journey, and like a wise traveler I've learned a few tricks along the way. I've learned just how strong faith can be. Along this road, I've learned about love and commitment, about forgiveness and about the resilience of the human spirit.

The more I learn of God and see His incredible handiwork in my little world, the more I believe in the certainty of destiny. I do not believe that things happen without reason or cause. There are no accidents. Every experience in my life led me to where I am today, and will direct me to whatever I have to face tomorrow. If you learn nothing else from these pages, know that God, working through me and through those around me, pulled me through the dirtiest fight of my life. He guided me to share what I know, to tell others that the fight is long but in the end you can win. I can smile and know that with Him in my heart and my home, I can always prevail.

I've learned that some questions can only be answered when you allow your spirit to be still. "How can I get through this alone? Where is God right now when I need Him the most?" It took me more than 30 years to realize He was right here with me all of the time. He put people in my path who helped me precisely when and how I needed them most. He put me with you. And He is with you right now reading this book. Trust Him and leave no box of blessings unopened in heaven.

Chapter Eight

What You Should Know

We stand at the precipice of a grave threat to our public health.... It affects all people from all walks of life, in every state, in every country. And unless we do something about it soon, it will kill more people than AIDS.

—C. Everett Koop, Former U.S. Surgeon General

These words are meant to inspire alarm and, indeed, over the course of this story, you may have felt vicariously overwhelmed by the enormous struggle required to fight hepatitis C. If you have been infected by this virus, you are not alone. It is suspected that around 4.5 million people in the United States are infected with hepatitis C and over 200 million internationally are infected. Liver failure due to hepatitis C is the leading cause of liver transplants in the United States.

In the preceding chapters you read about how hepatitis C affected Mark Prater physically and emotionally. The authors wish to devote this chapter to helping you to better understand the disease and its treatment. We will include conversations with the doctors who initially diagnosed Mark's disease and provide you with resources to learn more about HCV.

What Is Hepatitis C?

Hepatitis C is a virus that attacks the liver. It is made up of a string of genes (the basic building blocks of cell growth and function), sheathed in a coat of protein, and like all viruses is designed mainly to reproduce. A hepatitis virus attaches itself to the outer membrane of the liver cell, infects the cell, and thus allows the viral genes to take over the cell's normal functions to produce more HCV. This process weakens the liver cell, which may die in a matter of hours, but has in the interim produced thousands of viruses which will go on to infect other healthy liver cells.

Once infected, liver damage progresses slowly through four stages. In stage one, HCV causes inflammation of the liver. Though scar tissue may form, it does not generally hamper liver function. The liver is further damaged in stages two and three, increasing the amount of scar tissue. Enough healthy liver remains to continue to work properly. However, by stage four the patient has developed cirrhosis, in which scar tissue has decreased function almost completely or the liver has stopped functioning altogether. In many people it takes up to 10 years to move from one stage to the next. 80-90% of hepatitis C infections become chronic (lifelong) and lead to liver disease.

Who Should Be Tested for Hepatitis C?

The Centers for Disease Control and Prevention recommend the following persons seek testing for HCV:

• Anyone who has ever injected illegal drugs

• Anyone treated for clotting problems with a blood product made before 1987, when safer manufacturing methods were introduced, or anyone who received a blood transfusion or solid organ transplant before 1992 when better blood testing of donors became available

• Anyone notified that they received blood from a donor who later tested positive for hepatitis C

• Long-term renal dialysis patients

• Healthcare workers after exposures to HCV positive blood

• Children born to HCV positive women

• Anyone who has had unprotected sex with an infected partner.

How Can the Spread of Hepatitis C Be Prevented?

• Avoid donating blood if you have been exposed to HCV

• Cover open wounds with bandages

• Do not share razors, toothbrushes, manicure tools, or any other personal care items that might carry traces of blood.

• Take precaution with menstrual blood.

• Clean bloodstains with bleach

• Use latex condoms when having sex. The risk of transmission is low between long-term, monogamous partners, but discuss the issue with your partner to decide if condoms are acceptable to you both

• Warn healthcare workers who may be exposed to your blood about your condition

• If you are a healthcare worker, follow routine barrier protection, and safely handle needles and other sharps.

What Are the Side Effects of Treatment of HCV?

• Flu-like symptoms

• Depression

• Anemia

• Mood swings

• Rash

• Shortness of breath.

• Birth defects. Hepatitis C treatment should not be done during or just prior to pregnancy.

Mark's Doctors Speak Out

The two doctors primarily responsible for Mark's recovery recognize that in the fight against the silent epidemic, the most effective weapon is education. Dr. Carl Nechtman, M.D., an otolaryngologist in private practice in Birmingham, AL, and Dr. Michael Fallon, M.D., a respected hepatologist in practice at the University of Alabama at Birmingham's Kirklin Clinic, both agreed to interviews for this book.

CLC: *Dr. Fallon, please explain the most common ways to acquire HCV.*

Dr. Fallon: The two most common ways to acquire hepatitis C are blood transfusions and intravenous drug use, and these mechanisms probably make up the source for more than 90% of all patients. There are a number of less common or rare modes of transmission, including sexual transmission, occupational exposure in the health care field, tattoos, intranasal cocaine, body piercing, and transmission from mother to child by so-called vertical transmission (during birth).

Sexual transmission of hepatitis C is a major concern to many patients and is a source for acquiring hepatitis C. However, in stable monogamous relationships the risk appears to be less than one percent per year. In people with multiple sexual partners who have unprotected sex the risk is higher, although the magnitude of the risk is not well quantified. Barrier contraception with latex condoms can minimize the risk of transmission. Sexual transmission appears to be higher in people who are HIV positive, an event that may be due to the fact that the amount of hepatitis C virus is higher in the setting of immunodeficiency. In this setting, semen or vaginal fluid may have more HCV virus present.

There is a small subset of patients for which the source of hepatitis C infection remains unknown despite questioning. This group appears to be shrinking as we have gotten smarter about how the virus is transmitted. Also, the stigma of having hepatitis C has lessened and therefore people are probably a little more forthcoming about risk factors.

CLC: *Dr. Nechtman, what led you to believe that Mark Prater was infected with hepatitis C?*
Dr. Nechtman: Mark came in with a plethora of symptoms that did not completely add up. They're not uncommon symptoms, seen by a lot of different specialists. I initially diagnosed him with reflux and some rhinitis, which is inflammation of the tissues of the nose. But he was having drainage and sore throat and I figured at that point he had some standard conditions that are very common in hard-working individuals who don't watch their diet and don't keep those abdominal muscles as firm as they should. And

he does in fact suffer from those, but generally they don't cause the kind of fatigue he was having, nor are they as hard to control with what he was putting in as a pretty good patient effort to do those things. That was the clue that said to me there's something different about this particular patient. He was doing everything that I asked him to do and doing it as diligently as I thought he could do it at the time.

When all the symptoms don't add up I will generally run some basic blood work consisting of a complete blood count, a check of the electrolytes, and a liver function test. During the process, the liver function test came back mildly elevated. That generally can be for a lot of reasons. It doesn't just indicate hepatitis C. But when somebody comes back with elevated liver enzymes who has no other ongoing problems that you can clearly define and/or no gall bladder disease, no gastrointestinal tract disease, not a heavy drinker, not a drug user of any sort, then you start to think that there is something going on.

CLC: *Is there a standard therapy regimen for HCV patients?*
Dr. Fallon: The current standard therapy is pegylated interferon and ribavirin. The pegylated interferon is given as a once weekly injection and the ribavirin is given multiple times a day in pill form, both for up to one year.

Pegylated interferon is a modified version of the interferon that has been used over the last fifteen years to treat hepatitis C. Pegylation attaches the interferon to a large inert molecule which stays in the bloodstream longer and results in more sustained levels of interferon. From a patient's standpoint it is easier to take because it is given less often (weekly). The major side effects of interferon are flu-like symptoms, lowering of the platelet count and the white blood cell count, and mood changes including depression. One of the other things that interferon does is stimulation of the immune system so it can predispose people to autoimmune diseases: thyroid trouble, arthritis, and some skin diseases may develop or get worse during treatment.

Ribavirin alone does not have beneficial effects on hepatitis C infection. However, in combination with inter-feron it significantly improves the effectiveness of treatment. Ribavirin may contribute to some of the constitutional side effects of therapy, but its major potential side effect is hemolytic anemia, where red blood cells break up at a faster rate than they normally would, resulting in a drop in red blood cell counts. This occurs in about 20% of patients and it may range from mild to severe. Low red blood cell counts may cause weakness, fatigue, and shortness of breath.

When considering treatment with patients who have hepatitis C, education is critically important. I believe you can never really tell people too much about the potential side effects of treatment. People who are going to take treat-ment need to be prepared mentally for the challenge. If they learn about side effects and then don't experience them, they are ahead of the game. If they have significant side effects, then they are prepared and are better able to meet the challenge. Both physicians and patients must remember that no patient will respond to treatment unless they can complete the therapy. A number of simple measures can help, including giving patients ibuprofen or acetaminophen when interferon is given, and making sure they stay hydrated and scheduling injections to minimize effects on daily activities. Also, I watch people very closely for the development of depression and put 30% to 40% of the people I treat on antidepressants during treatment. Finally a host of additional side effects include itching, rashes, and other effects considered "minor" are very important to address. As physicians we may not consider them medically important but to patients struggling with multiple treat-ment-related symptoms they are extremely important. We need to be sensitive and responsive to each symptom and strive to address, minimize, or resolve as many treatment related issues as possible.

CLC: *Why is the spread of hepatitis called the silent epidemic?*

Dr. Fallon: The reason we have a silent epidemic is because the liver infection with hepatitis C tends to be low grade and may not cause a lot of symptoms. Therefore, people may go many years with relatively mild liver function test abnormalities and if they are otherwise healthy and have no other reason to see their doctor they may have a prolonged undetected infection. Over time, the low-grade inflamma-tion may lead to scarring in the liver, particularly if other factors that may injure the liver are present (including regu-lar alcohol use, weight gain with fatty liver). By the time sig-nificant symptoms develop and the infection is recognized, liver damage may be well established and in some cases advanced. In addition, hepatitis C may have been acquired through behaviors (intravenous drug use) or events (blood transfusions) that occurred in the relatively distant past and if patients do not tell health care providers or are not asked, testing may not be performed. Finally, the natural history of hepatitis C is in general prolonged, on the order of 10 to 40 years before substantial liver injury and symptoms are more likely to be present.

The good news is that new transmission of hepatitis C is not increasing. In fact, it looks like fewer people are getting infected. The reason that more cases of hepatitis C are being found is that with increased awareness and testing, more and more people infected over the last 30 years are being recognized. So the keys to controlling the spread of hepatitis C are detecting and treating patients with hepatitis C and avoiding exposure to potentially contaminated blood. From a public health standpoint our blood supply is the safest it has ever been in terms of screening for hepatitis C. In addition, common sense practices to reduce the risk of transmission, such as avoiding sharing razors and toothbrushes, practicing safe sex, and other recommendations that fall into the category of universal precautions against communicable diseases, are appropriate.

CLC: *Why is hepatitis C so difficult to treat?*
Dr. Fallon: Several issues contribute to the difficulty in treating hepatitis C. First, the notion of the silent epidemic plays a role; if the disease is not recognized until it is advanced, treatment may not work as well and there are more risks inherent in the therapy. Second, we are just beginning to develop better tests and more specific agents to clear the virus from the body. Third, hepatitis C presents vaccine developers with a real challenge. HCV can change its genetic makeup and it does so more rapidly than the HIV virus. These mutations affect the protein coat of the virus,

which is the marker the body uses to detect and fight HCV. Producing a vaccine is harder, therefore, because the virus is constantly changing its appearance.

CLC: *Are new cases of hepatitis C on the rise?*
Dr. Nechtman: I'm seeing more patients with hepatitis C. There are a couple of reasons for that. Probably the biggest reason is that we are specifically looking for it now. Twenty years ago, hepatitis C was probably a thought in some researcher's mind. It was thought to be extremely rare; we saw it in things like hemophiliacs or people who have had extensive blood transfusions. But there was really no specific test, much like the AIDS virus. When there's no test for it, how can you pick it up? As we become more cognizant of the fact that these folks are having symptoms, that they are having liver problems from chronic hepatitis C, researchers have developed tests to pick it up. Now, everything that comes through the blood bank is tested not only for AIDS and hepatitis B and a number of other things, they're screened for hepatitis C so you can hopefully prevent the spread of each virus. But more importantly, you've got all these people who are surviving this viral illness and we're seeing the after effects 10, 15, 20 years down the road. So we're able to see a longer natural history of the disease.

CLC: *Are there any new treatments on the horizon?*
Dr. Fallon: Yes, and steady progress has been made. One of the most important ongoing activities is optimizing the treatments we currently have. This includes testing and using different forms of interferon and of ribavirin and determining who to treat and how long to treat so that we

target and treat the patients who have a reasonable chance to respond. Although these efforts are not novel they are very important, because they are likely to have the greatest impact on the success of therapy over the next five years. There is also an enormous effort to develop novel animal and cell culture model systems to study how hepatitis C affects the liver and how the body responds to the infection. One of the problems in developing new treatments has been the lack of good animal and cell culture models of hepatitis C infection. The development of newer systems to look at how the virus works, how the immune system responds to the virus and how the virus escapes the immune system is playing a major role in designing new and more effective treatments. In addition, research into the specific mechanisms of transmission, infectivity and cell damage of other viruses is helping us understand more about hepatitis C. For example, much of what we have learned about HIV has been useful in developing treatments for hepatitis C.

CLC: *How do patients ensure that they are receiving optimal care in terms of diagnosis and treatment for hepatitis C?*
Dr. Nechtman: The scope and breadth of medical practice today prohibits anybody from being an expert in every field, so I'm forced to say there's too much knowledge out there for me to have a full command of it all. I'm forced to master my own field. Ideally, we would spend all day long with one patient, and then probably after reading and deliberating and going back and poking and probing, you could probably revive some old memories of going through the disease processes as you read through them between medical school and residency. But in reality you fix the people you can fix

the fastest and if it doesn't add up, generally those people get sent back to their family doctor who may or may not have any insight on where to go next. Sometimes deciding which fork in the road to choose is very difficult. Take someone with experience in the field of cardiology, for instance—if they've seen one heart attack they're more likely to recognize the next one. And so you want to pick someone who has the experience or at least has the insight enough to point you down the right road. A lot of symptoms Mark had get passed around from doctor to doctor, and had he not had any liver functions drawn they could have been mistaken for fibromyalgia, which is a very common diagnosis.

Patients may go to ten doctors and say, "Doctor so and so finally found it." This does not mean that the physician failed in his or her duty. The doctors may have answered the question that the referring physician asked of them. If they sent Mark to me and asked, "Does he have hearing loss, does he have reflux, does he have sinusitis?" and I say yes or no, then I've done my responsibility to my referring physician. The problem is, we're dealing with human beings and not just a car that you take back to the factory and everybody checks it on the assembly line.

Doctors don't walk on water. Doctors are people. The doctor patient relationship to me is a dialogue, not a dogma, not a dictatorship, and it's certainly not a sermon. With Mark, it didn't sound like all one disease process, something else was going on to push him down a little further and I questioned what I could do to expedite his recovery and more importantly get him to the right doctor. We're faced with a new realm of medicine where a lot of people feel more and more like machines. If the doctor takes your symptoms seriously then you've won the battle.

Taking Care of Yourself

When undergoing treatment, it is important to take care of your body to prevent health problems that could make hepatitis C even worse. Take these precautions to maintain a healthy lifestyle.

• Avoid alcohol. Your liver may be functioning at a reduced level, and drinking alcohol may make you more likely to develop cirrhosis.

• Be careful what medications you take. Some medications and supplements can be harmful to the liver and may exacerbate medical complications. Check with your doctor or pharmacist before ingesting any over-the-counter drugs, and make sure your doctor is aware that you have hepatitis C before he or she prescribes medication.

• Maintain a balanced diet. Eating the right foods can boost your immune system.

• Get plenty of rest. Your immune system also requires recharged batteries every day. An adequate amount of sleep may be critical to your recovery.

Find Out More

There are many organizations those infected with HCV and their caregivers can turn to for support and education. Here are some resources you can use to find out more about hepatitis C.

American Liver Foundation
1-800-GO-LIVER
www.liverfoundation.org

Centers for Disease Control and Prevention
1600 Clifton Rd. NE
Atlanta, GA 30333
1-800-311-3435
www.cdc.gov/hepatitis

Hepatitis Foundation International
30 Sunrise Terrace
Cedar Grove, NJ 07009
1-800-891-0707
www.hepfi.org

Office of Minority Health Resource Center
P.O. Box 37337
Washington, D.C. 20013-7337
1-800-444-6472
Fax: 1-301-230-7198
www.omhrc.gov